The Unity We Seek

The Unity We Seek

ROBERT RUNCIE

*Compiled and edited
by Margaret Pawley*

Darton Longman and Todd
London

First published in 1989 by
Darton, Longman and Todd Ltd
89 Lillie Road, London SW6 1UD

© 1989 Robert Runcie

British Library Cataloguing in Publication Data

Runcie, Robert, *1921–*
  The unity we seek.
  1. Christian church. Concepts: Community
  I. Title   II. Pawley, Margaret
  260

  ISBN 0–232–51788–6

Phototypeset by Input Typesetting Ltd,
Printed and bound in
Great Britain by
Courier International Ltd, Tiptree Essex

Contents

HEALING

Foreword

The first Lambeth Conference in 1867 and the twelfth in 1988 bear striking similarities. Both Conferences gathered at the invitation of the Archbishop of Canterbury. Neither possessed any executive authority over the Communion as a whole. Each convened at a time when the unity of Anglicanism was considered especially fragile. The ordination of women to the episcopate is the focus of that concern in our own day, but for the first Lambeth Fathers it was the heterodox views of Bishop Colenso which seemed to have consequences potentially as far reaching. They were accused of evading hard issues. So too were their successors in 1988 by some contemporary commentators. Yet Anglicanism has a special vocation to seek unity and to preserve and maintain it when it seems particularly brittle.

If there is a thread linking my addresses during the past year it is this theme of unity. How may unity between nations be fostered? That question broods over a reflection on Gallipoli which in itself reveals how frequently war brings men to a sense of their deep unity with one another and even with God. The address to the National Evangelical Anglican Celebration considers how our doctrine of the Church may unify many gospel imperatives. The opening of the healing centre in the crypt of St Marylebone Parish Church provided an opportunity to explore the unity which may exist between the Church's healing ministry, orthodox and alternative medicine. 1988 was also the year of the Russian Millennium. I was glad to celebrate the unity and integrity of this unbroken Christian tradition. The Kristallnacht commemoration illustrated a contemporary unity between Jews and Christians which, had it applied a half-century earlier in Europe, would have surely altered the course of recent history.

The range of issues upon which a modern archbishop is expected to speak makes him rely often upon the wisdom of others for inspiration and guidance. My small, dedicated and loyal staff give me cause for consistent gratitude in this area. Beyond them there lies a group of friends and confidantes whose ideas and suggestions are frequently employed in my own thinking, sometimes consciously, often unconsciously. I am indebted to them all. Margaret Pawley deserves a special note of gratitude for putting these addresses in order and vigilantly chasing sources which I failed to record at the time of writing.

It is, I believe, a privilege to be made to think about the issues in this book. I believe the quest for unity within the Church and the world is nothing less than the beginning of a pilgrimage towards the divine union which is God's vocation for us all. 'How lovely it is to dwell together in unity.'

UNITY

1

The Nature of the Unity We Seek

Since the first Lambeth Conference in 1867, the bishops of the Churches of the Anglican Communion have gathered at the invitation of the Archbishop of Canterbury every ten years (wartime excepted) to discuss and debate the key issues of the day.

The Archbishop addressed the 1988 Conference which comprised 525 bishops from all over the world. There were also many observers from other Churches. His theme was unity.

Let me begin with a homely illustration. My mother read detective stories – mystery stories, where the secret is revealed on the last page. But she had a habit of reading the last chapter first, thus seeing how it all fitted together. I follow her in turning your attention to the last chapters of the last book of the Bible.

In the Book of Revelation we are given a vision: a new heaven and a new earth, and the holy city, New Jerusalem, coming down from God out of heaven. Here is God's disclosure of the unity of the whole human family. The Lord God Almighty and the Lamb are the central focus of the holy city. All the nations shall walk in the light of the glory of God and of the Lamb. The Kings of the earth shall bring with them the glory and honour of the nations. *And the gates of the city shall not be shut* (cf. Rev. 21:22–7). Exclusiveness is not a characteristic of the City of God.

In this vision there is ultimately no difference between the quest for the Church's unity and the quest for human healing in the widest sense. The Church is the model towards which the whole human family will look for its healing and reconciliation. To the degree that the Church is effectively gathered in unity in the assembly of worship around God and the Lamb, it is the sign of hope and the bearer of good news to the whole world.

Neither the Church nor the world 'sets the agenda': God has *his* agenda of shalom, unity and communion. *We* must seek to be loyal to it. So the question of Christian unity always needs to be considered in the light of what it's *for*. What would be the value of unanimity without purpose? Human unity is the goal of God's mission to his creation – though in relation to the Lamb on the throne. Christian unity is part of our share in that mission, the sending of God's Son and his Gospel and his Church to the ends of the world.

But here is another picture. During the sunset years of European colonialism, a young British District Officer wrote to his fiancée in England describing the home in East Africa that he looked forward to sharing with her. 'From the hillside', he wrote, 'I see the smoke rising from the cooking fires in a dozen villages scattered along the valley; part of the forty thousand subsistence farmers who live all around. My nearest neighbours are three hours' drive away, but we usually meet for tennis once a fortnight.'

Nor is this limited definition of the neighbour peculiar to Europeans. I have been told a Ghanaian proverb which runs: 'The stranger who came says he saw no one in the town and those he met said they saw no one come.'

All talk of human unity, without the vision of the heavenly city wherein the nations walk, becomes an arrogant attempt to rebuild the Tower of Babel. Is this not the lesson of the rise and fall of empires both ancient and modern? And are we not seeing this re-enacted in the contemporary resurgence of nationalism and tribalism?

At this plenary assembly of the Lambeth Conference I see in so many of you the personal embodiment of God's mission to a broken and divided world. As Anglican bishops, bishops in full communion, and as ecumenical observers, you come with wounds humanity cannot by itself heal: the wounds of Southern Africa and Uganda, Sudan and Ethiopia; the wounds of the Philippines, Korea and Sri Lanka; of Nicaragua, El Salvador, Argentina; of Jerusalem and the Middle East; the wounds of Ireland; the great global wounds of distrust between East and West, and the increasing disparity between North and South. Look at each other as human beings bearing the marks of human brokenness. But look at each other also as fellow citizens of the heavenly city, and as those who worship the Lamb and who are thus constituted within Christ's Church as a sign of hope for the whole human race, the bearers of the gospel of reconciliation.

It is within this broad agenda, God's agenda for the unity of all creation, that we must set the no less divine agenda of Christian unity and the unity of the Anglican Communion. An ecumenical observer put this strongly at the meeting of the Anglican Consultative Council[1] in Singapore last year. All discussion of ecumenical matters, he argued, should constantly have in mind the *purpose* of the church as sign and sacrament of the Kingdom. 'It is', he said, 'only where people actually bleed and weep that their wounds can be bound up and their tears wiped away.' How can we see the heavenly vision and at the same time tolerate women and men, God's masterpieces, belittled by reason of their colour, sex, or social class?

It has been one of the great strengths of the World Council of Churches, whose fortieth anniversary falls this year, that it has always set the search for Christian unity in this wider context. From the days of a divided and shattered Europe after the Second World War till the present time, this has never been forgotten.

The structure of my address is dictated by this fundamental agenda. But we have to begin somewhere specific and concrete. Only when the burning glass is focussed is fire kindled. What story would Our Lord have told to that young District Officer in East Africa: surely the parable of the Good Samaritan, with its fundamental interrogation: 'Who is my neighbour?' At this Lambeth Conference we may well ask the same question ourselves. And the answer must be the fellow bishop

1. Anglican Consultative Council: an international body linking all the Provinces of the Anglican Communion composed of representatives of the twenty-eight autonomous Anglican Churches. All Churches are represented by a bishop, the larger ones may also be represented by a priest and/or a lay person. Its President is the Archbishop of Canterbury and it meets in different parts of the world once every three years.

who differs from us theologically, politically, or culturally, as radically as the Jew from the Samaritan. For a while bishops with deeply opposing convictions must live and debate and pray together as neighbours. We shall do this in the company of representatives of the world-wide Church through the presence of bishops in communion and the ecumenical observers. We shall be taking important decisions about our relations with other Churches and looking with some rigour at the goal of Christian unity.

So we begin where we are. I shall speak in what follows of unity within the Anglican Communion, of ecumenical unity among the Christian churches, and finally of the unity of all creation.

UNITY WITHIN THE ANGLICAN COMMUNION

I want to begin this section about unity within the Anglican Communion with a strong affirmation of gratitude. Our mood is eucharistic, in spite of the conflict and debate we must realistically anticipate. We give thanks to God for our communion with him and with each other as Anglican Christians. As I travel round the Anglican Communion I am filled with enthusiasm for what I see and hear, and especially for the people I meet at the local level.

I think of a Hispanic 'street' celebration of the Eucharist on the West Coast of the USA, praise and liberation not locked up in a sanctuary; of the consecration of four new churches on one boiling hot day in the outback of Australia; of the indomitable enthusiasm and valour of the Church in South Africa at Archbishop Desmond's enthronement; of the beauty and reverence of worship in Japan; and of the fresh idealism of young Anglicans at their meeting in Northern Ireland. Many of you could tell similar stories, especially from Partnership in Mission consultations and the regional preparatory meetings for this Lambeth Conference.

So I have had to say with some vigour to the British press of late that the Anglican Communion is not about to dissolve; and to the Church of England Synod that it is a little early to be taking the covers off the life-boats and abandoning ship.

So let us maintain the note of joy and thanksgiving with

which we began the Conference at the Eucharist yesterday and with which we begin each day. The ecumenical presence among us is also a sign of mutual confidence and trust. Our partners in the Gospel may have their problems with us, though they also say to us 'there are good things in the Anglican Communion'.

But I want to say too that we must never make the survival of the Anglican Communion an end in itself, the Churches of the Anglican Communion have never claimed to be more than a part of the one holy catholic and apostolic Church. Anglicanism, as a separate denomination, has a radically provisional character which we must never allow to be obscured.

One of the characteristic features of Anglicanism is our reformation inheritance of national or provincial autonomy. The Anglican tradition is thus opposed to centralism and encourages the thriving of variety. As in nature, you need some wild life as well as cultivation for healthy growth. There is an important principle to bear witness to here: that nothing should be done at a higher level than is absolutely necessary.

So Anglicans have become accustomed to speak of a dispersed authority. And we are traditionally suspicious of the Lambeth Conference becoming anything other than a conference. We may indeed wish to discuss the development of more solid structures of unity and coherence. But I for one would want their provisional character made absolutely clear; like tents in the desert they should be capable of being easily dismantled when it is time for the Pilgrim People to move on. We have no intention of developing an alternative papacy. We would rather continue to deal with the structures of the existing Petrine ministry, and hopefully help in its continuing development and reform as a ministry of unity for all Christians.

But Anglican unity itself is most characteristically expressed in terms of worship. Here we have much in common with the Eastern Churches, whose very name implies a unity through right worship – 'Orthodoxy'. This is a proper corrective to an over-institutional view of Christian unity and to an over-intellectual understanding of unity through assent to confessional formulae. In liturgical worship the Scriptures are proclaimed, the creed is confessed, the sacraments are celebrated, and all is given order through an authorized epis-copal ministry.

Nevertheless, I do not wish to sound complacent. There are real and serious threats to our unity and communion, and I do not underestimate them. Some of them are the result of Gospel insights: for example the proper dignity of women in a Christian society. I hope it will not dominate this Confer-ence, but we need to recognize that our unity is threatened over the ordination of women to the priesthood and episcopate in *whatever we ultimately decide to do*. There are dangers to our communion in this Lambeth Conference endorsing or failing to endorse such developments. And there are equal dangers to communion by trying to avoid the issue altogether. Such conflict is particularly painful, because the glue which binds us together is not so much juridical, but personal, informal and expressed in worship. An impairment of communion for Anglicans is not essentially about canon law but at the much deeper personal level of sharing in the eucharistic worship of the Holy Trinity. So we tend to shy away from a conflict which has such destructive potential. This is of course a serious mistake.

We need to recognize the persistence and place of conflict in Christian history. There has never been sharper conflict among Christ's people than the great debate over the admis-sion of the Gentiles to the Church without the ceremonial law. Think of Paul withstanding Peter to the face (Gal. 2:10).

Nor were the early ecumenical councils of the Church any easier: tempers blazed on the doctrines of the person of Christ and the Holy Trinity, charge and counter-charges were lev-elled, coalitions were formed. At the Council of Ephesus the monk Shenouda hurled a copy of the gospels at Nestorius – a gesture at once orthodox and effective, for it struck him on the chest and bowled him over.

Yet in and through such unholy conflict the Church eventu-ally, and never without difficulty, came to a common mind. Through the initiatives of prophets and primates, the deliber-ations of synods, and the active response of the whole Church, the Holy Spirit has been at work. Conflict can be destructive. It can also be creative. We are not here to avoid conflict but to redeem it. At the heart of our faith is a cross and not, as in some religions, an eternal calm.

The creative use of conflict is part of the process of discerning the truth. As the Rabbinic scriptures put it: 'controversies for the sake of heaven'. This is not to propagate polemics but to explore truth. There is a constant dialogue here between revelation and culture in every age. Tradition is not archaeology but the contemporary expression of 'the faith which was once delivered unto the saints' (cf. Jude 3). Consistency with Scripture and continuity with the past there must be. But this does not entail the mere duplication of the past.

So the Church has a living tradition which develops and grows in the tension between that which has been given and the present experience of the community. At the Lambeth Conference the Anglican Communion tries to discern what is of the Spirit, and what is not, and to express this in a living voice. Conflict, then, far from being an unmitigated evil, is, if handled creatively, an essential part of our understanding of the processes whereby the Church speaks with a living voice today. T. S. Eliot said after the 1948 Conference, 'The Anglican Church washes its dirty linen in public; but at least it gets washed.'

In any case the problem that confronts us as Anglicans arises not from conflict over the ordination of women as such, but from the relationship of independent Provinces with each other. Although we have machinery for dealing with problems within a diocese and within a Province, we have few for those which exist within the Communion as a whole.

Another reason for looking critically at the notion of the absolute independence of Provinces arises from our ecumenical dialogues with world-wide communions. These require decision and action at more than provincial level. And our own experience as a world communion also teaches us the importance of a global perspective at a time when political concerns for 'national security' often militate against international co-operation and diminish the significance of world organizations such as the United Nations.

The New Testament speaks more in terms of *interdependence* than *independence*. The relationship of Jesus with the Father in the bond of the Holy Spirit, as witnessed in St John's Gospel, surely gives us the pattern of Christian relationship. Life together in communion implies basic trust and mutuality. Think of Paul speaking of life in the Body in his first letter to the Corinthians: 'The eye cannot say to the hand, "I have no need of you," nor again the head to the feet, "I have no need of you." ' (1 Cor. 12:21). The good of the Body requires mutual recognition and deference in Christ. Or think of Paul's collection for the saints in Jerusalem, a practical expression of communion on the theological ground of unity in Christ.

The idea of interdependence is not new to Anglicanism. The Toronto Conference of 1963, which gave us the slogan 'mutual responsibility and interdependence in the Body of Christ', also gave birth to the whole Partners in Mission process. But the full consequences of such mutual responsibility and interdependence have hardly yet been realized. It has taken the conflict over the ordination of women to point up the implications for the Communion. Here is powerful illustration of the fact that conflict has creative potential.

It can be put this way: are we being called through events and their theological interpretation to move from independence to interdependence? If we answer 'yes', then we cannot dodge the question of how this is to be given 'flesh': how is our interdependence articulated and made effective; how is it to be structured? Without losing a proper, but perhaps modified, provincial autonomy this will probably mean a critical examination of the notion of 'dispersed authority'. We need to have confidence that authority is not dispersed to the point of dissolution and ineffectiveness.

Should our answer be 'yes' to a minimum structuring of our mutual interdependence, that which is actually *required* for the maintenance of communion and no more, we would in fact be challenging the alarming isolationism and impatience I detect on both sides of the debate about the ordination of women. We would challenge not only the 'go it alone' attitudes of enterprising independence, but also the 'I and only I am left' attitudes of those who believe they are the sole repositories of 'true' Anglicanism.

Let me put it in starkly simple terms: do we really *want* unity within the Anglican Communion? Is our world-wide family of Christians worth bonding together? Or is our paramount concern the preservation or promotion of that particular expression of Anglicanism which has developed within the culture of our own province? Would it not be easier and more realistic to work towards exclusively European, or North American, or African, or Pacific forms of Anglicanism? Yes, it might. Cultural adaptation would be easier. Mission would be easier. Local ecumenism would be easier. Do we actually need a world-wide communion?

I believe we do, because Anglicans believe in the one holy catholic and apostolic Church of the creed. I believe we do, because we live in one world created and redeemed by God. I believe we do, because it is only by being in communion *together* that diversity and difference have value. Without relationship difference divides.

This is why I have called the present Lambeth Conference. This is why I have visited many of the Provinces of the Anglican Communion in solidarity with both your joys and your sufferings. I have tried to be a personal and visible presence of the whole Anglican family in places like the Province of Southern Africa, where solidarity between the world-wide Church and particular Christians is a gospel imperative if ever there was one.

So I believe we still need the Anglican Communion. But we have reached the stage in the growth of the Communion when we must begin to make radical choices, or growth will imperceptibly turn to decay. I believe the choice between independence and interdependence, already set before us as a communion in embryo twenty-five years ago, is quite simply the choice between unity or gradual fragmentation. It would be a gentle, even genteel, fragmentation – that much of Englishness still remains – and it would not be instant. As I have said, the Communion is not about to disappear tomorrow. But decisive choice is before us. Do we want the Anglican Communion? And if we do, what are we going to do about it?

ECUMENICAL UNITY AMONG THE CHRISTIAN CHURCHES

When we turn to unity among the Churches we have similar hard questions to ask; for there is a feeling that the ecumenical

movement has run into the sand, and there is a lassitude and
scarcely veiled apathy about unity discussions. A prominent
English spiritual writer has called ecumenism 'the last refuge
of the ecclesiastical bore'.[2] Certainly there have been ecumenical failures to account for the evaporation of the enthusiasm
of a generation ago. And Anglican Churches have been prominent in all parts of the world, except the Indian sub-continent,
for failing to endorse national unity schemes.

But my answer to ecumenical apathy is to say, Look at the
local scene. The more encouraging sign of ecumenism in the
last few years in many parts of the world has been the startling
growth of local covenants and areas of ecumenical exper-
iment. There is the Interim Eucharistic Sharing agreement
between Anglicans and Lutherans in North America. Perhaps
I can also be allowed to give a British example of local
ecumenical initiative – a process called 'Not Strangers But
Pilgrims'. For the first time Christians of almost all the Churches are working together to find ways of expressing their
unity more visibly. This includes black-led Churches, the
Roman Catholic Church and Orthodox Churches, as well as
Anglicans and Methodists, and Reformed Churches. Couple
this local activity with the achievements of the various theological conversations between the Churches, and it is hard to
sustain objectively the view that ecumenism is in the
doldrums.

But there is a certain hostility to the idea of Christian unity.
The very process of ecumenical discussion raises the question
of what each partner believes. The issues of the *identity* of
separate churches is sharpened. I like to tell the story of the
old Scotsman who became more and more agitated at the
time of the Anglican-Presbyterian unity discussions some
years ago. He would not have bishops in the Scots Kirk. His
family could not understand this. 'But father,' they said,
'you're an atheist.' 'Aye,' he replied, 'but I'm a Presbyterian
atheist.' My answer to this is to agree that ecumenism is a
risk. We risk the loss of *denominational* identity in the search
for *Christian* identity; what C. S. Lewis meant by 'mere Chris-

2. Harry Williams CR.

tianity'. Ecumenism is not in fact a threat to our identity but its enlargement.

An additional consequence of this anxiety about identity is that we may be tempted to rest content with *denominational federalism* rather than the catholic diversity of the coming Great Church. Agreement in faith, it is argued, is impossible to achieve, nor does the New Testament give warrant for it. For communion in faith we must substitute the coexistence of radically different styles of faith and ecclesial life. Instead of visible organic unity grounded in agreement in faith it would be better to lower our sights and work for the lesser goal of a federal ecumenism.

But does New Testament diversity license us to settle for coexistence? I would argue that this view fails to take account of the development of 'catholic' structures within the New Testament itself. The pastoral Epistles witness to a recognition of the need for bonds of unity to hold the diverse Christian communities together. Such a view fails to take account of the significance of the canon of Scripture, which declines to parcel out diversity in separate containers and insists that 'all things are yours'. Thus we are not called to choose between Johannine and Pauline Christianity, but are called to be confronted and enriched by both.

There is need here to attend carefully to the evangelical contribution to ecumenism. For, despite the doubts of Evangelicals about structures and ministries for unity, I look forward to a major contribution from them because of their unwavering and biblically grounded conviction that there is One Lord and One Faith. This is itself a wholly constructive critique of the position of those who simply want to rest content with pluriformity. And from the conviction of One Lord and One Faith we shall all then be able to advance to the consequences of the recognition of One Baptism; the visible unity of the One Church.

Another important evangelical insight, derived from the Reformation, is that the Church is in constant need of renewal. The Church exists for the Gospel and not for itself. We would all want to acknowledge the achievements and growth of contemporary renewal movements. I recently

attended a SOMA[3] gathering; SOMA is powerful in charismatic enthusiasm and remains eager to be loyally Anglican.
I applaud their loyalty to our Communion and their longing
for the renewal of the whole Church in the freshness of faith.
There are many groups like them, in all the Churches, who
are in revolt against cerebral, institutional religion and, to be
frank, against some of the ingredients of this lecture and my
recipe for unity: they feel themselves already one in the Holy
Spirit.

My hesitations are that such movements can tend to sit in
judgement on the institutional Church. It is safer, it is said,
to stick with 'real' Christians! But it was Luther himself who
said that you needed the Church to preach the Gospel in the
first place. Furthermore, such attitudes leave little room for
the seeking pilgrim. The student who said, when asked to
give his whole life to Christ, 'I still know so little of my own
life and need to know so much more of the Christ to whom
I am to be committed', should not be lost to the Church. We
need commitment, yes, but expressed in a variety of styles:
some enthusiastic and emotional; others questioning and
intellectual; yet others through traditional rite and ceremony.
This brings me again to the question of diversity.

In my strong reaffirmation of the vision of *one* Church I
hope it is no longer necessary to stress that unity is not a
synonym for uniformity. Though we would be naive to sup-
pose that we are the only comprehensive Church, it has been
a particular characteristic of Anglicanism to stress diversity.
Without diversity the body cannot flourish, grow or develop.
If diversity is not fostered, schism ferments.

Fundamental to the unity of the Body of Christ is our
common confession of Jesus as Lord. Subordinate to this are
a number of visible signs of the existing communion between
the Christian Churches which institutional schism has
impaired, but not altogether taken away: the confession of
one apostolic faith revealed in the Scriptures and set forth in
the Catholic Creeds; the practice of one baptism with water
in the name of the Trinity; a common concern for the poor
and powerless, manifesting itself in a community of resources;

3. Sharing of Ministries Abroad.

an acknowledgement of shared goals and values derived from the belief that humanity is created in the image of God; and a common commitment to the apostolic mission Christ has entrusted to his Church.

All these are largely and widely shared by the ecumenical community. They point to an existing unity between the Churches. But for full ecclesial communion, for the fullness of the unity we seek, this existing unity requires development and embodiment. This brings us inevitably to the structures which will serve both the unity and diversity of the Church.

One such instrument of unity is the *historic episcopate*. But here Anglicans have to be very careful to commend episcopacy without the negative overtones, which Christians of 'non-episcopal' Churches have so often heard. I hope our discussion of Anglican-Lutheran relations and the Lima text[4] can be the context for a new affirmation of the value of episcopacy as a sign of the apostolicity of the whole Church, the continuity of the Christian community in time and space. 'No "unchurching" and no denials of the experience of any Christians need accompany the firmest insistence on Episcopacy,' wrote Michael Ramsey.

Another is the *council or synod*. From the beginning of the Church it has been necessary to come together for conference debate and decision. Here I am particularly anxious that we listen to the voice of the Orthodox Churches for whom synods and councils have such an important place. I was present at the recent Synod of the Russian Orthodox Church, and I was humbled by the reminder that their first modern Synod (of bishops, clergy and laity) took place in 1917, rather before my own Church of England, though not of course before many of the Churches of the Anglican Communion.

It would be good if there could be some conversation between our Orthodox observers and the bishops from Africa, because I am struck by some similarities in the way in which decisions are reached. In an Orthodox Synod much emphasis is given to the achievement of moral consensus. In the African tradition this is also the case. The synod will debate an issue

---

4. World Council of Churches document on Baptism, Eucharist and Ministry.

until there is a common mind and the decision will only then be taken.

In other parts of the Anglican Communion we have developed a more legalistic attitude to councils. In the Church of England, when a decision is about to be taken in Synod, the Registrar calls 'Divide': the very word for schism and the exact opposite of the true meaning of 'synod', to come together.

If we still have some things to learn about synodical government I also believe we have something to give to the Church of Rome. For me the major criticism of the Anglican-Roman Catholic International Commission[5] must be its lack of emphasis on the role of the laity in the decision-making of the Church.

As Anglicans we are trying to learn how conciliar bodies such as this Conference, the Primates Meeting and the Anglican Consultative Council all relate together. We should be particularly glad to welcome the Anglican Consultative Council's full presence among us, as we explore how we maintain our unity together. As bishops we bring our diocese with us. But we also need the special-interest groups the ACC can represent.

To bishops and councils I would also want to add *primacy*. ARCIC puts before Anglicans the question of an episcopal primacy in the Universal Church: an instrument of unity we have been lacking since Henry VIII's juridical break with Rome in the sixteenth Century. Not all Anglicans view the restoration of such an office with equanimity. ARCIC, it must be remembered, is not proposing *restoration* but a *reform* of primacy as a ministry of unity.

In October 1986 I visited Assisi at the invitation of Pope

5. Anglican-Roman Catholic International Commission (ARCIC): the official body constituted to conduct the international theological dialogue between the Churches of the Anglican Communion and the Roman Catholic Church. The dialogue was established in 1967 after Archbishop Michael Ramsey's visit to Paul VI in Rome in 1966. The first Commission (ARCIC-I) published a number of Agreed Statements on Eucharist, Ministry and Authority. The second Commission was established by the present Archbishop and Pope John Paul II in Canterbury in 1982. It continues to work on the outstanding theological problems between the Anglican and Roman Catholic Churches.

John Paul to pray for peace with Christians ranging over the whole Christian spectrum. And alongside Christian leaders were representatives of all the great world religions. That Day of Prayer for Peace was something I had wanted to see since Pope John Paul made his ecumenical pilgrimage to Canterbury Cathedral. We spoke of the idea then and I gave it all the encouragement I could. Whether we like it or not, there is only one church, and one bishop, who could have effectively convoked such an ecumenical gathering.

At Assisi I saw the vision of a new style of Petrine ministry; an ARCIC primacy rather than a papal monarchy. Pope John Paul welcomed us, including other Anglican primates present here at this Conference, but then he became, in his own words 'a brother among brothers'. And at the end we all bundled into the same bus and the Pope had to look for a seat.

Our own Anglican experience of belonging to a world communion also points to the need for a personal focus of unity and affection. Of course a Canterbury primacy is very different from the kind of sovereignty which has been exercised by the popes for many years. But could not all Christians come to reconsider the kind of primacy exercised within the Early Church, a 'presiding in love' for the sake of the unity of the Churches?

In serving the Gospel, and thus the unity of the Church, *bishops, synods* and *primacy* are structures in radical need of reform and renewal. But we must beware of an ecumenical idealism which prefers to wait around until episcopacy, synods or popes are exactly as we would have them. Renewal then would become an excuse for inaction, a retreat from committing ourselves to each other as we are. It would be like a perpetual engagement in which marriage was for ever being postponed until the partners were perfect. No, the way to perfect your partner is to enter a new and more intimate relationship so that mutual change comes by intrinsic desire rather than extrinsic demand.

As with the Anglican Communion, so ecumenically: we must move from independence to interdependence. And the same question necessarily arises: 'Do we want unity?' I do, because our Lord prayed for it on the eve of his passion. I do, because our Lord prayed for it in the context of mission: 'That they all may be one . . . that the world may believe.' I do, because neither conflicting Churches, nor competitive Churches, nor coexisting Churches will be able to embody effectively the gospel of reconciliation while the Churches themselves remain unreconciled. Do we Anglicans *really* want unity? We must do if we are to be instruments of unity and communion to a divided world.

THE UNITY OF ALL CREATION

This leads me to that wider ecumenism which is the original meaning of *oikumene* with which we began. I have not ventured into inter-faith dialogue because I am conscious that this address is directed to those who can respond tomorrow. But a comprehensive coverage of my title would certainly demand from me something of the encounter with world religions. It will be an important part of the Conference agenda. For me all people of faith, all those with spiritual awareness, possess potential for greater unity through dialogue, though fellowship, and the service of the wider community; that is why I went to Assisi.

I make no apologies, however, for spending time on unity among Anglicans and with fellow Christians. It would be hypocritical to avoid our particular domestic problems for the sake of a rhetorical concern for global unity, about which this conference can itself *do* very little.

Indeed, the penitential recognition of the fragmented nature of the Christian family may usefully prevent us from glib talk about human unity which only too easily slides into secular optimism and the discredited liberal notion of inevitable progress. To speak (in the language of our conversations with Reformed Christians) of the Church as the sign, instrument and foretaste of the Kingdom is *not* to be equated with utopianism.

I was reminded of this vividly in Moscow recently. There is an obelisk in the Kremlin near the Tomb of the Unknown Warrior commemorating the forerunners of the Revolution. It includes the name of Thomas More, the author of *Utopia*. The trouble with earthly utopias is that, by leaving out God, they take short cuts: 'All men are brothers except those who in the name of brotherhood need to be eliminated.' It is a remarkable fact that when men leave out the heavenly city they cannot build a tolerable city on earth.

Yet, though the Kingdom is not susceptible of political arrangement, the Christian leader cannot escape specific political questions. If bishops keep to the safe paths of moral generalities, they are dismissed as impractical idealists. If they chance their arm and venture social comment, they are accused of technical incompetence and political interference. We cannot win. Here I believe the Churches need to listen to each other's experience. The older Churches can learn much by sharing in the debate of the younger Churches about 'liberation theology'. Not that Kingdom imperatives will mean the same solutions in each place, but that we must all bring a gospel critique to our respective societies.

Christians have particular insights. Because their ultimate vision is of the Kingdom of God, of men and women caught up in the divine interdependence of the Holy Trinity, they are unlikely to rest content with any existing political arrangements. The *Christian* vocation is to live in society, in communion. And so the search for communion among Christians gives us a pattern for the wider communion of all humanity.

I have glimpsed this among Christians in many different parts of the world. I think of a eucharist in a Lutheran church in Dresden, East Germany, that was totally destroyed by Allied bombing in the Second World War. There were hundreds of young people in the congregation. I was invited to assist in the distribution of the sacrament, and as the people received communion some whispered, 'Thank you for coming,' or the like, after their Amen to the Blood of Christ. Here was the Church of Jesus Christ transcending the man-made political divide between East and West.

In India I was able to meet Mother Teresa of Calcutta. In her home for the dying she was washing out the ward. She put down her bucket, took my hand, and looked deeply into my eyes. As someone said, she makes you feel big and small at the same time; but what I had not realized was that the home for the dying is built on temple ground. The temple is dedicated to the heathen goddess Kali, from whom the city

of Calcutta derives its name. Here is the Church giving Easter
hope, peace and dignity to the dying next door to a temple
of a pagan goddess of death and destruction.

Again, an AIDS clinic in San Francisco supported by the
Episcopal and Catholic Churches embodies the same gospel
message of love, pastoral care and hope. You, too, will have
stories from your own Churches of the Church as a model of
what it is to be human.

But the unity God intends does not fall short of the *whole*
creation. Someone said recently: 'Preoccupation with the
human is beginning to sound distinctly parochial.' Kiev, which
I visited recently, the cradle of the Russian Church, is not
far from Chernobyl. Perhaps because of this, one of the Metropolitans stressed the urgency of a serious Christian discussion
of environmental and ecological issues. Scientists today would
also wish to stress the 'interdependence' and balance of
nature, rather than a misunderstood, competitive, evolution-
ary theory. So I would want to urge strong Anglican support
for the World Council of Churches in their preparation for
the World Conference on 'Peace, Justice and the Integrity of
Creation'.

Early in 1988 I was in Australia for their bicentennial
celebrations, but I visited the Aboriginal peoples as well as
those who had arrived more recently. I went to the Northern
Territory and worshipped with Aboriginal Anglicans. We
shared a fellowship meal in the open air: a kind of communion
with God, each other and the earth. I also saw a remarkable
relationship between a progressive mining company, the
Church, and the Aborigine community. Whereas in the past
the aboriginal people and the environment had been
exploited, *now* there is co-operation and partnership: a living
example of that interdependence between humanity and
creation which is the Creator's plan.

I am reminded of a prayer of the Ojibway people of
Canada:

> Great Father,
> Look on our brokenness,
> We know that in all creation

Only the human family
Has strayed from the Sacred Way.

Great Father,
Holy one,
Teach us love, compassion and honour,
That we may heal the earth
And heal each other.

I began with the Heavenly City. If you go on to the final chapter of Revelation you will remember that the River of the Water of Life flows through the city and on either side there is the Tree of Life. A garden city, an echo of that original paradise of the first book of the Bible in which, under God, Man and Woman are the gardeners of creation.

It is our conviction as Christians that in Jesus Christ (himself once mistaken for a gardener), we come to share in the New Man, the Second Adam, the renewed humanity. It is the task of the *one* Church of Jesus Christ to embody more visibly this new humanity as Good News for all people and all creation. Let me end with two verses from the Epistle to the Ephesians, the Epistle of Unity, which brings all this together:

For [God] has made known to us in all wisdom and insight the mystery of his will, according to his purpose which he set forth in Christ as a plan for the fullness of time, to unite all things in him, things in heaven and things on earth (Eph. 1:9–10).

This is the unity Christians seek.

2

The Christian Vision

On the first Sunday morning of the 1988 Lambeth Conference, the Archbishop gave the address at the inaugural Eucharist in Canterbury Cathedral.

I do not cease to give thanks for you, . . . praying that you may know the hope to which he has called you, the riches of your inheritance in the saints, and the greatness of his power in us who believe. (Eph. 1:16, 18–19)

These words I give you from the Scriptures: unceasing thanksgiving for our fellow Christians; gratitude to God for the hope to which he has called us. These are foundations of the Christian life.

I give unceasing thanksgiving to God that I have been privileged to see so many dioceses and countries in the past eight years; I have celebrated the Eucharist amid ice in the Arctic and in coconut plantations in the tropics. The Anglican Communion is emphatically international.

I thank God that we form a *Communion*: not an empire, nor a federation, nor a jurisdiction, nor yet the whole Church, but a communion; a fellowship based on our gathering at the Lord's Table, where we share 'the means of grace and the hope of glory'.

We come together so that this Communion can be known by us in a real and personal way as we meet face to face. We come to share, to learn, to listen, and then to search for words that will guide and encourage our Churches. We come expecting God to do great things, in us and through us and in spite of us. The Anglican Communion has its joys – enormous growth in some parts of Africa,[1] for instance – but it has its heartaches too. We must not let immediate needs, no matter how pressing, restrict our Christian vision to the present. God calls us, insistently, consistently to be people of the future, *his* future.

Such was the assurance of the writer of the letter to the Ephesians. These verses are but part of a sustained, even breathless, vision which gathers momentum, never pausing until that last majestic sentence: 'Now unto him that is able to do abundantly above all that we ask or think according to the power that worketh in us, unto him be glory in the Church by Christ Jesus, throughout all ages, world without end. Amen' (Eph. 3:20–1).

Why should the writer be so optimistic? He is suffering; he is in prison; he is helpless. But in his weakness he knows that something much greater is going on, something much greater than any observer of human affairs might detect – God's purpose is coming to fulfilment.

In Canterbury Cathedral the visitor's eye is caught by its massive pillars. In their strength they seem to stand on their own feet, symbols of strong foundations and sturdy independence. Yet their strength is an illusion. Look up and you see the pillars converting into arches which are upheld, not by independence, but through inter-dependence. 'An arch', wrote Leonardo da Vinci, 'is nothing else than a strength caused by two weaknesses; for the arch in buildings is made up of two segments of a circle, and each of these segments being in itself very weak desires to fall, and as one withstands the downfall of the other, the two weaknesses are converted into a single strength.'

We do well to remember that human weakness and our dependence on each other are not things to overcome, but gifts to offer to God as he works out his purpose in the world. To this place came St Augustine fourteen centuries ago. He came to plant the Church of Christ amongst the barbarous people of Angle-land, and there seems little doubt he came in great apprehension. Who, according to the world's reckoning, would have thought that he and his few companions would

1. 175 African bishops attended the 1988 Lambeth Conference.

survive in the midst of a sometimes savage paganism? But this great cathedral – standing at the place to which Augustine came with fear and trembling, in human weakness, but in the power of Christ – stands as a witness to the 'immeasurable greatness of his power in us who believe' (Eph. 1:19).

Other Churches have similar stories to tell, many of them much more recent. Think of Andrew Kaguru and the martyrs of Kenya, killed by the Mau Mau in the 1950s for refusing to attack white people. Or think of the riches of our inheritance from martyred bishops such as John Patteson[2] in Melanesia or Janani Luwum[3] in Uganda. Who now believes Idi Amin more powerful than Janani Luwum, who died for a faith he might have shared with us at the last Lambeth Conference? Who now believes Pontius Pilate more powerful than Jesus Christ?

God *does* confound expectations and transform tribulation into triumph *in his own time*. The time-scale of God's purpose is not known to us, but there is evidence enough that the vision expressed in my text is not a dreamer's fantasy but a prophet's declaration of the truth. It sees human activity and the witness of the Church to Jesus Christ in a divine perspective and upon a divine time-scale. So must we.

Ten years pass between Lambeth Conferences – no time at all in the divine perspective but a seemingly long time in our rapidly changing world. Some of our past leaders are no longer of our company, though assuredly they are with us in the Communion of Saints. I think of Michael Ramsey,[4] learned and holy; Festo Kivengere,[5] a winning evangelist; Gregory Hla Gyaw,[6] often isolated, never unsupported, in Burma; Moses Scott[7] and Erika Sabiti,[8] pioneering post-colonial leadership; Lakshman Wickremesinghe[9] of Sri Lanka,

2. 1827–71; first Bishop of Melanesia, murdered 1871.
3. Archbishop of Uganda, murdered 1977.
4. Archbishop of Canterbury 1961–1974.
5. Bishop of Kigezi, Uganda, 1972–1988.
6. Bishop of Rangoon and Archbishop of Burma 1979–1987.
7. Bishop of Sierra Leone and Archbishop of West Africa.
8. Bishop of Kampala and Archbishop of Uganda, Rwanda, Burundi and Boga-Zaire.
9. Bishop of Kurunagala, Sri Lanka, ?–1981.

fearless in opening eyes to fresh promptings of the spirit; and John Armstrong's ministry of reconciliation in Ireland.

If some of the hopes of the last Lambeth Conference have remained unrealized, so also have some of our worst fears. I have seen recently something of the remarkable developments in the Soviet Union. Those who have kept alive the resurrection faith see new horizons. And within China we have witnessed the recovery of Christian life; no, more than that, the development of a truly Chinese Christianity. All these things are cause for unceasing thanksgiving. But they must be set against an enduring and even escalating gap between rich and poor nations, the malevolent misuse of what should be blessings of technology, intensified racial strife, and human arrogance in the exploitation of the natural order. There is no cause for facile optimism.

Even so, my experiences around the world have taught me not to make an even more facile mistake. Amongst the desperately poor, the technologically undeveloped, and the educationally deprived I have often found a richness of spirit and a depth of trust in God which puts many Western Christians to shame. Being well fed and well housed and well educated, is no proof of a healthy spirit, a depth of faith or insight into God's purposes. When *things* take us over we live increasingly restricted in the present moment.

In such an atmosphere Christians must again look to their Lord and his example. There is a sense of urgency, even of immediacy, in the ministry of Jesus and his Apostles. 'Behold, now is the accepted time; now is the day of salvation' (2 Cor. 6:2). That temptation to postpone difficult decisions, which we ourselves know so well, does not receive much support in the New Testament record. The boldness of the present moment does often seem to be a good part of our obedience to the Holy Spirit, and if we retreat from it we should not be surprised if there is a dimming of the vision we once had.

Yet at the same time, this urgency has nothing of frantic insecurity about it; it is born not of fear, but of faith. We are taught to live with what is partial, fragmentary, provisional, even dangerous, *because* we believe there is fullness in Christ, the fullness of God's purpose for his creation, the fullness of undefeated love. And trusting in that providence we are able to live bravely in the present, picking ourselves up again after our manifest failings and mistakes. A church will never learn from its mistakes unless it is ready to risk making some. We can live with our human weakness for, even when we may be confined to a short view ourselves, God's perspective is long. The Church lives always under the light of eternity which Christ has shed upon her.

Here in Canterbury Cathedral, as I think of these things, there comes vividly before my mind a glimpse of the light of eternity shed upon us by Michael Ramsey, to whom we said our earthly farewell as his coffin lay before St Augustine's throne. He was always teaching us to see the journey of Jesus towards the Father and his journey into the darkness of the world as a single pilgrimage towards God in adoration and towards the world in service. As for Jesus, so for the Christian; not two journeys but one.

I can think of no better prayer for the Lambeth Conference than that we let ourselves be taken deeper and deeper towards God in adoration and, inseparably from that, deeper and deeper into the needs of humankind.

It is this perspective I want to commend and encourage. Whilst we ought not to be self-important in a foolish way or expect the walls of our particular Jerichos to fall flat at the blast of a few Lambeth resolutions, neither ought we to be dismayed by the tasks before us. Let us simply commit ourselves to Christ, as we are, to do what we can together and to leave the issue to that power which is above all that we can ask or think.

For we may be sure of this: important though the Lambeth Conference is, crucial though it may seem to the well-being of the Anglican Communion, nevertheless in the range of God's purpose it is no more than a small ship sailing on a wide, a very wide ocean. We must guide that ship as best we can. But in the end its destination and that of our Communion will not be determined by our skill and diligence as navigators but by the power of that all-sustaining, all-embracing, ever-flowing and ever gracious purpose of God in this his beloved world.

3

The Close of the Lambeth Conference

The final session of the Lambeth Conference ended on 6th August 1988.
In the early part of his closing address the Archbishop testified that
the Conference had for him created spiritual energy and fresh vision.
He touched on areas of the conference which had helped to create energy,
and he gave thanks to the many people who had contributed to it in
many and various ways, recognizing that 'gratitude to God is always
made flesh in thanks-giving to people'. He continued:

We have been reminded again and again of the obligations
of our common life. We have been faced with the imbalance
of our world's resources. Whilst Christians in the West often
seek to discipline themselves to a simpler life-style in the
midst of affluence, for Christians elsewhere in the world it
is often material poverty which is the foundation of their
evangelical simplicity. Of course we know that the poor may
be spiritually wealthy, but we should also face the hard truth
that the imbalance of our different Provinces' resources too
accurately reflects the imbalance of the world's wealth as
well. The obligations of common life mean we should do
something about it.

Common life, that is what we have *experienced* here, a
common life which lies at the heart of communion. There has
been much talk about being 'in' or 'out' of communion, about
'full communion' and 'impaired communion'. But the communion we have known together is something other, something far, far deeper. It has begun in the daily awareness of
that 'wonderful exchange' in the words of the Eucharistic
Prayer we have so often used from our worship book, the
exchange in which God takes and transfigures what is ours

and we receive what is God's. From that encounter each day
at the Lord's Table there flows a pattern of life together that
is itself a 'way of exchange'.

Our communion here has not been a quiet blending together, like sleepy little streams trickling into some big pool. It
has been the vigorous meeting of persons, with both their
ideas *and* their hopes and passions. It has not been without
conflict, because persons of flesh and blood inevitably move
in and out of conflict and grow through it. Most of all it has
been joyful discovery; the discovery of a common treasure
despite our diversity.

Another good thing about the Lambeth Conference is that
we meet as *equals*. I believe our capacity to see Christ in the
experience, the praying and thinking of others has grown
daily here. Once we all recognize each other as gifted with
Christ's grace, we become incapable of thinking them trivial
or ineffective. Remember Archbishop Desmond's words about
how we should be ready to genuflect to each other as carriers
of Christ. We should *reverence* each other; reverence for God
that leads to reverence for his people and creation; reverence
for his people and creation that leads to reverence for God.

Our priority as a Church is, I believe, to discover how we
might 'give thanks for each other', as one of the section
groups expressed it. St Paul gives thanks to God for the life of
communities which he violently disagrees with, as in the first
chapter of the first letter to the Corinthians, as well as those
he warmly approves of, as in the beginning of his letter to
the Philippians. This mutual thanksgiving is the life blood of
communion. It is how 'the wonderful exchange' of God's life
and ours continues to be real for us.

Canonical questions about what is or what is not 'full
communion' are important but I would say: 'Remember to
test all this language finally by the standard of the *reality* of
communion; the joyful and grateful showing of Christ to each
other that has happened daily here.'

When we have met to study the Bible; when we have met
at the Lord's Table; when we have shared in fasting and vigil;
when we have wept together over the pain of Southern Africa
or the Pacific (and there have been *real* tears shed, make no
mistake); have we been in 'full' or 'impaired' communion?

However real the difficulties those words represent, there is sometimes something almost laughably inappropriate about the question. Do not lose sight of that as you return to your dioceses. Our communion is real but it is not for our own enjoyment; it is for a purpose. That purpose is to look towards the Lord Jesus as he leads us into what seem impossible tasks. Some have thought this Conference was impossible. Reason and experience suggested we would fall apart. But keeping our eyes on the Lord we have not sunk.

I am reminded of a sermon Pastor Niemoller[1] preached over thirty years ago at Cambridge. He told the story of Peter walking on the water. He observed that when Peter kept looking towards Jesus he could do that of which human potential seemed incapable, but when he looked away he began to drown. Let Niemöller, that prophet, pastor and guide of a persecuted church, have the last word:

> As long as the church lives only for herself, as long as Peter does not leave the boat, she lives safely and undisturbed . . . but when the Church goes forth into the surrounding world and bears witness to the truth, then it becomes clear that her existence is just as impossible as that of her master himself. And yet we are challenged to lead the same impossible sort of life as Christ did, obeying God rather than man and loving our enemy rather than trying to destroy him. That, indeed, means danger instead of security, risk instead of safety . . . [Jesus] wants his Church to continue his work in the midst of a raging and stormy world, which nevertheless is longing for his reconciliation and peace, and which can be helped only by a Church not afraid of an impossible existence and task, but trusts in the call and promise of her living Lord!

1. Martin Niemöller, 1892–1984; German anti-Nazi Lutheran theologian, imprisoned in a concentration camp 1937–45.

4

The Anglican Communion

In the wake of the Lambeth Conference the Archbishop established a commission under the chairmanship of the Most Reverend Robin Eames, Archbishop of Armagh. Its purpose was to study the relationship between the various Provinces[1] of the Anglican Communion and how communion might be maintained between them.

The need for this commission arose from the possibility that a woman might be ordained to the episcopate,[2] and for the need for guidelines which would maintain communion between the Provinces, despite varying practice. In his address[3] to the commission, the Archbishop offered some personal reflections on the mandate given to it by the Lambeth Conference.

I have been empowered by a Resolution[4] of the Lambeth Conference, and consultation with the other Primates,[5] to invite you to come together to consider the relationship between the Provinces of the Communion and to offer pastoral

1. Province: a group of dioceses forming an autonomous Anglican Church, e.g. the Church of England or the Church of the Province of Southern Africa. As with Primates, there are historical exceptions. But in normal Anglican Communion usage the term Province applies to the whole Church.
2. This subsequently happened early in 1989 in the Episcopal Church in the United States of America.
3. Given on 23 November 1988.
4. See note on page 34.
5. Primate: the senior bishop in a province. Some Anglican Churches have more than one primate for historical reasons, but in Anglican Communion usage the term normally refers to the senior Primate only, e.g. the Church of England has two primacies in the Archbishops of Canterbury and York.

guidelines. That Resolution called for respect and courtesy while also recognizing differences of principle and an impairment of communion. You are inevitably going to have to deal with pain and hurt of both sides of this debate, as the Resolution itself recognized. But I would not have you forget the context of the Resolution of the Lambeth Conference itself. You were present at the Conference and in spite of our differences, sometimes deeper than we imagined, we experienced a remarkable sense of living in communion which no document or report can adequately embody or convey. That experience of communion in Daily Office and Eucharist, at table and in debate, and especially in our common Bible study is more important than any resolution or description of ecclesiastical relationships. I hope and pray you may be aware of this as you do your work together, for you are remembered in the prayers of the whole Anglican Communion.

My second reflection is related to this living experience of communion. I believe you would do well to consider some form of introduction on the nature of communion. I am not thinking of an elaborate theological study: this is the task of the Inter-Anglican Doctrinal Commission and ecumenical conversations such as the Anglican-Roman Catholic International Commission. But if you are to assist Provinces which differ on the ordination of women to the episcopate to maintain 'the highest degree of communion', you will need to offer some explanation of the notion of 'degrees' of communion. I have already tried to tell the General Synod[6] of the Church of England that it is not a matter of simply being in or out of communion. We need to think more in the ground between what is canonical and what is a matter of private judgement. I have also reminded the Church of England that communion in the earthly Church must always fall short of the fullness of the communion of the Kingdom of God to which it imperfectly

6. General Synod: the national Synod of the Church of England composed of elected representatives of the clergy and laity and the ex-officio membership of the diocesan bishops. It is in effect the Church's parliament and passes canons directly to the Crown for royal assent and other church legislation via parliament which can however only exercise a veto. It meets three times a year under the presidency of the Archbishops of Canterbury and York.

points. I believe some such introduction may help to put any limitation of communion in perspective.

Next you will, I believe, have to state with as much clarity and charity as you are able the actual position of the various Provinces as far as these are known. This is not to say that Provinces will have permanently fixed positions. The Resolution recognizes that there is a continuous process of reception which includes other churches as well as the member churches of the Anglican Communion. Yet you will need to know the position of Provinces now if you are both to describe and enhance relationships between them. Part of an honest description of where Provinces stand will be to state the actual canonical position of each Province with regard to a woman bishop and those ordained by her. I have tried to do it so far as the Church of England is concerned. Even that is not so easy when you are handling terms which others wish you to translate into theological questions of validity or regularity and see how they might then affect future legislation. It seems to me that there are probably three positions to be considered: the legal, the theological and the spiritual reality.

As to the two latter, I said to the General Synod of the Church of England that my statement of the canonical position must not be confused with a final theological judgement upon the spiritual fruitfulness of the ministry of a woman bishop. We are long used as Anglicans to making distinctions of this kind in relation to the ministries of other churches whose ministry of word and sacrament we would not wish to deny, even if their ministry is not interchangeable with our own.

Then you are explicitly asked by the Lambeth Conference to offer pastoral guidelines to the Provinces. These guidelines must, I suggest, embody both the letter and the spirit of the Resolution. They will be designed to foster the 'respect' and 'courtesy' the Conference called for. But they must not compromise the difference of 'principles' of which the Resolution also spoke. Clearly such guidelines will need to touch on visiting bishops and clergy as well as the question of invitations to the consecration of a woman bishop. This has some urgency and I would appreciate guidance from this meeting; I have already been faced with questions on the matter in the General Synod of the Church of England. As Archbishop of Canterbury I would also hope for particular advice on what Provinces should expect of me when I am invited to visit them. My office belongs to the whole communion. Yet I must also respect the integrity of the position of my own Province. You might also wish to consider the question of the development of local unity schemes with the Roman Catholic Church. There is also the question of firm advice on the undesirability of participation in the consecration of bishops for so-called 'continuing' churches.

Finally, I hope you will be able to devote some thought to how we can strengthen the bonds of communion between the Provinces. If you are able to offer guidelines which foster respect and courtesy and yet do not impugn deeply felt matters of principle, you will have already done much to build up communion in love and truth, in spite of some restriction of communion in ministry. We need to continue to reflect on ways of deepening our communion together, of extending the Lambeth experience of living communion, especially in the area of common decision-making. This is not simply a matter of strengthening the significance of the Primates' meeting, but of considering other steps which have been recommended. The Pastoral and Dogmatic Section at the Lambeth Conference has already set us thinking about this, stimulated by Archbishop Eames' work in the Anglican Consultative Council[7] on a common Declaration of Assent. Perhaps this needs to be supplemented through means by which serious matters of faith or order are referred to Provinces for obligatory consultation. You are faced with finding out the stance of the Provinces. I think of the analogy of Provincial reference to dioceses before a final decision on important matters.

These are some thoughts which occur to me as I consider your difficult task. While I do not underestimate the magnitude of your responsibilities, I am encouraged by the conviction that the vision that we saw at the Lambeth Conference was no mirage. I do not believe the Communion is about to disintegrate over this issue. On the contrary, I have the hope that we may actually discover something *more* of the meaning

7. See chapter 1, note 1.

of communion as we learn from our experience. You have a vital role to play in discerning and articulating this deeper communion. May God the Holy Spirit lead you into the riches of his truth as you thus serve the unity of the Anglican family in this Commission.

Resolution 1 of the Lambeth Conference, 1988:

THE ORDINATION OR CONSECRATION OF WOMEN TO THE EPISCOPATE

This Conference resolves:

1.   That each Province respect the decision and attitudes of other Provinces in the ordination or consecration of women to the episcopate, without such respect necessarily indicating acceptance of the principles involved, maintaining the highest possible degree of communion with the Provinces which differ.

2.   That bishops exercise courtesy and maintain communications with bishops who may differ, and with any woman bishop, ensuring an open dialogue in the Church to whatever extent communion is impaired.

3.   That the Archbishop of Canterbury, in consultation with the Primates, appoints a commission:
(a)   to provide for an examination of the relationships between Provinces of the Anglican Comunion and ensure that the process of reception includes continuing consultation with other Churches as well;
(b)   to monitor and encourage the process of consultation within the Communion and to offer further pastoral guidelines.

4.   That in any Province where reconciliation on these issues is necessary, any diocesan bishop facing this problem be encouraged to seek continuing dialogue with, and make pastoral provision for, those clergy and congregations whose opinions differ from those of the bishop, in order to maintain the unity of the diocese.

5.   Recognizes the serious hurt which would result from the questioning by some of the validity of the episcopal acts of a woman bishop, and likewise the hurt experienced by those whose conscience would be offended by the ordination of a woman to the episcopate. The Church needs to exercise sensitivity, patience and pastoral care towards all concerned.

5

Human Survival

In his address to the Global Forum of parliamentary and spiritual leaders, a major international conference held in Oxford in April 1988, the Archbishop showed a deeply felt concern for the earth's dwindling resources, damaged and reduced as they have been by man's greed and exploitation. He testified to his belief that only through world co-operation could our planet and its inhabitants continue to exist.

I am always rather hesitant in using the term 'historic' to describe occasions such as this. Like Herodotus, the father of history, we can never confidently predict how a future generation might judge our efforts. So I hope you will allow me to think of this Forum as 'historic' in a more limited sense of that term.

In October 1986 at Assisi, many with spiritual responsibility gathered to pray for peace. These leaders came from very diverse religious traditions. At other times and in other places there have been significant gatherings of religious leaders, statesmen, scientists and those representing the arts. Like all of these, this Forum too is clearly one of those occasions when leaders in different areas of life can come together to reflect upon the urgency of their own *historical* predicament. It takes place at a time when, in secular terms, it is not just human survival but the whole earth which is in some evident peril. In spiritual terms, these are times which *challenge* all those who believe there is a transcendent dimension to life and who believe in the ultimate sovereignty of the Good. Either way we are confronted by problems which transcend national and credal boundaries, which are urgent and potentially terminal, and which require no less than a global sol-

ution. We live in a world society which desperately seeks
some measure of world community in order to survive.

What spiritual resources can be brought to bear upon this
situation? First, and most self-evidently, we can bring our
faith: that is our awareness of the transcendent. We must
regard this, whatever its source, as an essential constituent of
being human, and recognize that all religious traditions affirm
the spiritual nature of humanity and recognize the 'divine
spark' in all human beings. Attempts in this century to eliminate this aspect of human nature have been markedly unsuc-
cessful. We must learn to affirm together the centrality of the
spiritual in our various traditions and that the unity of all
human beings is grounded and crowned in an ultimate unity
which is greater than the recognition of it in each of our
traditions.

We are still learning about sharing at the material, economic and social levels; it will surely help us to realize that we
need to share at the spiritual level too. We need, as never
before, to share our different spiritualities with each other.
Our world is in danger of being pervaded by a widespread
pessimism about the future of humankind. There is a diminished sense that our problems can be resolved by technology
alone or political utopias alone. We are confronted by a search
for meaning in the human enterprise, the need for reconcili-
ations, for greater compassion, for justice and for a celebration
of life in all its wholeness. These are deeply religious themes.

There are many among those who stand outside the major
religious traditions who have an unfulfilled longing for salvation, for spiritual fulfilment. There are others who are seeking for a 'golden core' of religion not confined to any specific
tradition but reflected in all of them. Then there are those
who feel that the world is in desperate need of a new and
larger vision of unity which transcends existing differences.

There are dangers here, as well as hope. In a recent lecture,
'On the Pursuit of the Ideal', Sir Isaiah Berlin drew a distinction between the quest for a perfected and unified world – a
good and noble pursuit – and the temptation to translate this
vision into reality by taking short cuts. Sir Isaiah chillingly
recalls that this temptation forms the genesis of each and
every final solution. So we are warned not to think that

resistance to our goal is always mistaken. There are genuine differences in the apprehension of truth. Ignorance and mal-evolence are not to be imputed as the characteristics of those who disagree with us. That is why dialogue is *so* important, not least in the sphere of religion.

All people of faith, all those with spiritual awareness, pos-sess potential for seeking greater unity through dialogue, through bonds of fellowship and through service of the wider community. This is why I am certain that the communion experienced in the sharing of our respective faiths – an element of central concern to this Forum – is ultimately about new relationships where we no longer see each other simply as competitors but as partners in a continuing dialogue about the meaning and purpose of life. This is not to say, however, that we endorse the views of those who hold that all religious traditions have the same core. Each tradition has its own distinct origins, doctrines and rituals which need to be respected and studied for what they are. For my part, I am bound to say as a Christian that definitive apprehension of the divine occurs in an encounter with Jesus Christ.

However, the recognition of religious traditions as distinc-tive does not necessarily involve us in the view that each tradition is strictly autonomous and is 'closed in' on its own history, doctrines and ethical emphasis. Rather, a willingness to enter into dialogue will recognize that religious traditions, although distinct, *are* accountable to each other and are open to public scrutiny in terms of values and truths universally recognized as basic to society. Such a 'mutual reckoning' must form a significant part of inter-religious dialogue.

One aspect of such 'mutual reckoning' in the context of dialogue might be the question of religious freedom in our respective societies. Do we, as religious people and as parlia-mentarians, encourage respect for those with different beliefs? Do we work for all to have freedom of worship and freedom in the practice of their faith?

The question of religious freedom brings to the fore the wider matter of our common commitment to basic human rights as set out, for example, in the United Nations Declar-ation on Human Rights. Matters such as these are not extra to the agenda for inter-faith dialogue but are at the very centre of it, for they involve our particular views on the nature of revelation, on the divine ordering of society, on development within a religious tradition and many other crucial matters.

As became clear at Assisi, at the world day of prayer for peace, inter-faith dialogue is not just a necessity for mutual religious understanding, but also a catalyst for the discussion and resolution of global issues. We began to see how as partners in religious dialogue we could begin to address major issues of world-wide concern. We sensed how our separate faith communities could begin to speak and act together on such major social issues as peace, poverty, the urban crisis and the scourge of AIDS; I might add today, acting together against that terrorism which fouls and feeds on global communications. We need to go on acting in concert for two very good reasons. One is that in our global village we have to work increasingly alongside creeds and cultures which are not our own, and with which we were previously unconnected. These are the people of our planet, and they will not go away. That is the new reality of our situation. Secondly, it is clear to me that all the religious traditions present here today, both the broader rivers and the smaller tributaries, are necessarily concerned with the whole of life: the secular as well as the sacred, the familial and well as the political. They possess not only spiritual insight, but also philosophies and ethical systems, significant elements of which have the potential to enrich the whole human race.

In theory that is; for in practice they have rarely fulfilled their secular potential, either individually or collectively. Too often, religious diversity has been disruptive of community, and it remains the root cause of tensions and deep divisions between different human groups. It is premature to presume that the age of holy wars is long past. The twentieth century has seen much bloodshed where religious differences have been a fundamental factor. It continues to do so, and each faith, far from transcending its own particularity in this respect, continues to be maimed and poisoned by the effects of sectarian conflict. At the same time, the forces of secularization are as destructive to authentic spirituality as those of this kind of religious particularism. Their net effect is to isolate religions as a minority cult, as a kind of spiritualized group therapy for the select few, and to transform them into what Professor John Bowker[1] has called 'inoffensive options which lie at the edges of life'.

We must reject such a privatization of religion which results in its reduction to being simply a matter of personal salvation. Nor can we accept the despair of those who would interpret the various crises we face today in the political, economic and ecological areas of life as the harbingers of the end of the world. The fatalism inherent in such a philosophy has no part in authentic religious awareness. Our awareness of crises in creation and in the human family should lead us, rather, to repentance and to a renewal of our commitment.

How therefore can our faith, both private and public, shared and yet unique, really speak to a world in crisis? This is of course a leading question with which you will be wrestling throughout this Forum. Let me leave you some spiritual reflections – I hesitate to call them guidelines – which may help you, whether your starting point is religion, or parliamentary affairs.

One is that beneath our shared urgency and shared hope today must surely lie a shared belief in the *orderliness* of the universe. It is precisely to this order that the ancient Greeks alluded when they called the universe 'cosmos'. In my religious tradition, belief in God as Creator is linked to a belief in the divine maintenance and government of the world. We believe in a God who provides providential care for his Creation. Pervading our tradition is the conviction that there is an all-wise power who rules the world for a sublime purpose. In different ways we confess that wherever we are, we are protected by God who watches over us, who expresses parental care for all his creatures, who has included our every step in his plan of Creation and who apportions the lot of humankind according to his own wisdom and goodness.

Such a belief in providence does not imply that God is the only actor in history. Human beings are not animated puppets. God has given us free will to act. Just as the world depends on God for its existence, so too does Creation depend

1. Dean of Trinity College, Cambridge, since 1984.

upon human activity. 'Creatureliness' was the term Baron
Von Hügel[2] coined more than half a century ago to describe
our right relationship to God in all this. God has granted
human beings the skills to further his creative purposes. In
this sense the doctrines of 'Creation' and 'Human Responsibility' for God's world are inextricably linked in my tradition.
God who is creator, sustainer and providential guide has
conferred upon human beings the obligation to join him in
the work of creation.

But joining God in the work of creation is not only our
vocation but our temptation too. The temptation is that we
will usurp God's place as Creator and exercise a *tyrannical*
dominion over creation. But are we to accept that the rest of
creation has been created only for us? Does dominion necessarily lead to domination? And what, in any case, are the
limits of the category of creation known as humanity?

At the present time, when we are beginning to appreciate
the wholeness and inter-relatedness of all that is in the
cosmos, preoccupation with humanity can seem distinctly
parochial. We need now to extend the area of the sacred and
not to reduce it. It may be that cosmologies which have arisen
out of certain Eastern traditions will enable us to appreciate
the significance and the value of the non-human in a new
way. The non-human parts of creation would then be seen
as having an intrinsic value of their own rather than being
dependent for value on their relation to human beings.

I believe that all too often our theology of Creation,
especially here in the so-called 'developed' world, has been
distorted by being too man-centred. We need to maintain
the value, the preciousness of the human by affirming the
preciousness of the non-human also, of all that is. For our
concept of God forbids the idea of a *cheap* creation, of a throw-
away universe in which everything is expendable save human
existence. The whole universe is a work of love; and nothing
which is made in love is cheap. The value, the worth of
natural things is not found in humanity's view of it but in
the goodness of God who made all things good and precious

2. 1852–1925; Roman Catholic theologian, author of *Mystical Element of
Religion*, 1908.

in his sight. Common action on moral and ethical matters begins in what we believe the world to be, in who made it and why. As Barbara Ward[3] used to say, 'We have only one earth. Is it not worth our love?'

I have ventured into such theological territory because I believe that people of all faiths share sufficient common ground to recover for humankind two necessary qualities for our survival.

The first is *reverence*. How can we prevent peoples and communities tearing themselves apart by racial strife or religious bigotry? How can we prevent creation being ravaged and exploited and polluted by human greed? How can we prevent the most intimate of human relationships being trivialized or distorted by pornography or promiscuity? How can we maintain respect for truth when our airwaves are choked with hateful propaganda?

Are not these, at root, questions of reverence for life, for people and for the physical environment? There is a need to recognize that modern technico-scientific culture is as affected by human sinfulness as any other area of human activity. Greed, hedonism and the lust for power are sometimes the forces which impel technological and scientific progress, culminating in the exploitation of the earth and its people. Tribal and aboriginal people have often been the victims of such hubris. In my travels over the world, I hear stories about how such people have lost their land and had their social fabric destroyed in the name of progress and development. Yet it is often the traditional world-view of such people which provides a framework for living in harmonious ways within the created order. There is a sense of the sacredness of the environment in many tribal and aboriginal communities. Such societies offer an understanding of the world which is based on the inter-relatedness of the human and the non-human, the animate and the inanimate. There is a need to control the hubris which impels much developmental activity and to reiterate that it is not only in the satisfaction of our elemental needs that human happiness is to be found. True

3. Dame Barbara Ward (Baroness Jackson), 1914–81; British writer and economist.

development, as a recent encyclical by the Pope points out, must be 'measured and oriented according to the reality and vocation of man seen in his totality, namely, according to his *interior dimension*'.[4] Stewardship of the earth and its resources is an important part of human vocation. For Christians and for very many others, reverence for the created order is only held to be secure in our reverence for God, the Creator of all.

The second and related quality necessary for our survival is *co-operation*. Competition is nowadays often seen as the mainspring of human activity. But I do not believe that our religious faith allows us to be content with an idea that self-interest is the only driving dynamic of human progress.

The distinguished Cambridge biologist, Professor Patrick Bateson,[5] challenges the idea that you can draw from the Darwinian theory of evolution the belief that the *only* thing which matters for progress in social or animal life is conflict. Mutual trust, co-operation, protection of the weak play their part. This is not the place to develop this theme in detail; I simply offer two quotations:

> The danger of representing all human social relationships in terms of competition is that the expectation is self-fulfilling. Trust is poisoned.

> Involvement with others occurs in every aspect of our lives. We should denounce the view that this is merely constraint on individual ambition. Co-operation should be seen for what it is – an essential and pleasurable part of being human.

For us, at any rate, it is more than that. We believe that we are fellow workers with God in the working out of his purposes for the world. 'The mother and nurse of pride', said a wise man long ago, 'is ignorance of God.'

Our common commitment to reverence and co-operation would provide the sure foundation for our future responsibility together in both spiritual and political leadership. I pray that we can share a readiness to listen as well as to say our piece.

4. Encyclical on Human Development.
5. In an article in *Theology*, Jan. 1986.

6

The Anglican Evangelical Movement

At the third National Evangelical Anglican Celebration, the Archbishop addressed nearly 3000 men and women,[1] lay and clergy, from this increasingly significant and vigorous wing of the Anglican Church.

Outside my study door in Lambeth Palace hang portraits of Archbishops Randall Davidson[2] and Cosmo Gordon Lang.[3] Between them they held my present office for roughly the first forty years of this century. I can find no record of either of them being invited to address a conference of evangelical clergy and laity. The reasons probably lie in that crippling diagnosis of the state of evangelicalism in the first half of this century once offered by Jim Packer.[4] He discerned 'archaic theology, spiritual conceit, ecclesiastical isolationism, social unconcern, pessimism about the world and the Church'.[5] But faults there were on both sides. The Church of England at the time scarcely welcomed any overtures from evangelicals seeking involvement in its wider life. I grew up in Liverpool where there were three ghettoes, High Church, Low Church and Modernist. The boundaries between them were firmly fixed.

Since then evangelicals have changed. The National Evangelical Anglical Celebrations have reflected this change as

1. At Caistor, on 29 April 1988.
2. Archbishop of Canterbury 1903–28.
3. Archbishop of Canterbury 1928–42.
4. James Innell Packer; Principal, Tyndale Hall, Bristol, 1970–7; Professor of Historical Theology, Regent College, Vancouver from 1979.
5. *The Evangelical Anglican Identity Problem: an Analysis*, Latimer Studies, no. 1, Oxford 1978.

well as causing it. One thousand attended Keele;[6] two thousand came to Nottingham;[7] the attendance here at Caister – may be something nearer three thousand. It was at Keele that an image was changed, and it was a product, let us remember, of the 1960s.

It is commonplace nowadays to belittle the Church of the sixties and its concerns. This was the age when the world set the agenda; when social work was prayer; when one clergyman declared, 'I would rather be called relevant that reverend'. Heady excitement followed the Second Vatican Council[8] when the liberation of the Roman Catholic Church seemed to have no foreseeable end. Anglican evangelicals were affected, like all others, by this ferment. The choice was either to retreat still further into a pietistic rejection of change or to risk the release of those evangelical energies which had for so long been kept in close confines cherishing the faithful.

The conference at Keele was a catalyst of change. It reaffirmed the authority of Scripture but at the same time was prepared to challenge all else in the light of Scripture, even the most cherished evangelical traditions. John Stott's[9] leadership was crucial and I am glad to note the tribute paid by David Edwards to John in the recently published *Essentials*.[10] Only William Temple, in David Edwards' view, ranks as a more influential clergyman in the Church of England in this century. We praise God for John's remarkable ministry. If we look back upon Keble's Assize Sermon in 1833 as the moment when the Oxford Movement began, so too Keele in 1967 was the birth of a new evangelical movement *within* the Church of England. The 'within' in that last sentence is important, for Keele did two things.

First, it affirmed *Anglican* evangelicalism. There had been a tendency for evangelicals in the Church of England to see more in common with those who share similar views in other denominations than with their fellow Anglicans. The estab-

6. April 1967.
7. April 1977.
8. 1962–5.
9. Rector of All Souls' Church, Langham Place, London, 1950–75.
10. David L. Edwards and John Stott, *Essentials*, Hodder and Stoughton 1988.

lishment of the Church of England Evangelical Council in 1960 marked the beginning of a new identity, both Anglican and evangelical, needing to apologize for neither description.

Secondly, alongside that firmer identity there came a new *openness* to other traditions and this was gladly reciprocated. Other traditions became more open to evangelicals too. For it was almost as if putting aside the insecurities and narrowness of the past had created firmer foundations for a dialogue with others in the same Church and outside it. The value of ecumenism, liturgical change, social action and sacramental life were central to the statements that followed those three brief days at Keele. An agenda was set which was pursued with remarkable faithfulness in the next decade. At Nottingham in 1977, similar sentiments were expressed. In the more sober atmosphere of the late 'seventies the excitement was not quite so heady, but the achievements of the previous decade for Anglican evangelicals were not to be swept aside. And these achievements were many: revitalized worship, especially musically; a mushrooming of youth organizations; publications like *Third Way*;[11] social action, both local and national; a new confidence and flair in evangelism. The list could go on, for the changes and the renewal were extensive.

The twelve-point Declaration of Intent which followed the second National Evangelical Anglican Celebration was a remarkable statement of corporate resolution in mission, witness and ecumenism. It also possessed that rare quality, corporate confession of past mistakes, failures and shortcomings. Repentance ceased to be something to which other people alone were called.

There are two extracts from that Declaration of Intent which I want to pick up as pointers to the future. One appears in the preamble; the other is significant because of its substantial absence.

In the preamble to the Declaration it says, 'We thank God for our evangelical heritage in the Church of England.' I am glad that found a way in. A little while ago Professor Henry Chadwick[12] said that 'a Church which loses its memory

11. An evangelical periodical published monthly.
12. Regius Professor of Divinity, Oxford, 1959–69; Cambridge, 1979–82; Master of Peterhouse, 1989.

degenerates into senility'. There was a time when evangelicals in the Church of England constantly looked back to great heroes of the past, lamented their passing and thought that their insights were as immutable as the text of Scripture. I sense that such a time is now long past. Perhaps liturgical change and charismatic renewal have distanced all of us from a sense of indebtedness to past Christian leaders. If so, that would be a great loss.

Recently a candidate for ordination, a graduate school master and a charismatic evangelical but, hopefully, quite untypical, told his Director of Ordinands that in his opinion the Holy Spirit had not been alive in the Church from the time of the completion of Scripture until the charismatic renewal of the 1960s. A modest study of Church history would, one hopes, enlighten him. I cannot, though, imagine that any evangelical of a previous generation would have been so dismissive or ignorant of the Reformation or the Impact of the Wesleys let alone the achievements of the Evangelical Revival in the Church of England at the end of the eighteenth and the beginning of the nineteenth centuries.

The most remarkable testimony to the impact of the Evangelical Revival came in an article which Charles Smyth[13] wrote during Second World War. He said:

> Within an incredibly brief space of half a century, the evangelicals, although a minority, converted the Church of England to foreign missions, affected the abolition of the slave trade and slavery and initiated factory legislation and humanitarian reform, healing the worst sores of the industrial revolution. Has any church in Christendom achieved so much in so short a time?

And that was not all. Personal conversion, family prayers and hymn singing were signs of a search for holiness. Whilst the later Oxford Movement transformed the Church, the impact of the Evangelical Revival on England was arguably much greater.

Smyth reminds us that these men were a minority in the

13. Fellow of Corpus Christi College, Cambridge; in 'The Evangelical Movement in Perspective', *Cambridge Historical Journal*, vii,3.

Church of England. It is perhaps foreign to the nature of
leaven to be numerically in the ascendant. Charles Simeon
sensed this. His influence from his Cambridge pulpit and in
his rooms in King's College, where his sermon classes were
held, spread far beyond the university city and its students.
But he did nothing to make evangelical clergymen extra-
parochial or super-parochial. He was insistent that they kept
to their parish boundaries as he kept to his. A large measure
of Simeon's influence in the Church of England came from
his belief in the complementary character of Church and
Gospel. The Church was not merely a useful organization for
the propagation of the Gospel. It was integral to the process
of sanctification. 'As for Simeon,' wrote Lord Macaulay, 'if
you knew what his authority and influence were, and how
they extended from Cambridge to the most remote corners of
England, you would allow that his real sway over the Church
was far greater than that of any primate.' That's a chastening
assessment for any Archbishop of Canterbury to remember.

There were two pointers to the future from the 1977 Nottingham Declaration of Intent. The first concerned the thankfulness for the evangelical heritage in the Church of England.
The second centred on what seems to me a notable absence
from the document, any strategic ecclesiological thinking.
There are hints of it here and there but no developed evangelical ecclesiology, and it seems to me that if the current evangelical renewal in the Church of England is to have a lasting
impact then there must be more explicit attention given to
the doctrine of the Church. So it is to that doctrine, commonly
called 'ecclesiology', that I now turn.

Michael Saward[14] has written:

> If I have one anxiety today about the Anglican evangelical
> movement (and others share it) it would be 'Will the
> numerical development ever bother to try to influence posi-
> tively the Church of England?' When one has worked for
> three decades to bring what one believes to be the beneficial
> influences of a biblical evangelicalism to bear upon the
> Church, at every level, it is sometimes discouraging to feel
> like a commando, who having landed in Normandy on the

14. M. Saward, *Evangelicals on the Move* (Mowbray 1987), p.73.

night before D-Day, looks out to see the army descending
on the beaches in daylight, only to be told that they have
decided to sing choruses on the beach at Bognor because
it's much more satisfying!

If this is an accurate diagnosis I do not believe it is the result
of sheer indifference and disinterest. It is the practical out-
working of a doctrine of the Church which takes the local
church seriously but sees wider bodies as bureaucratic, organizational and political rather than an expression in themselves
of the Body of Christ.

I believe this is mistaken and not evangelical. Let me illustrate what I mean from Scripture, since our doctrine of the
Church must begin in the New Testament. There we find an
extraordinarily rich imagery for the Church which already
developed in the first few vibrant years of the primitive
church's life: Church and Gospel are inseparable; the mes-
sianic community, the bride of Christ, the new Israel, the
body of Christ. These are not organizational or institutional
images; they are pictures of the Church wrapped up in the
very message of the Gospel.

Let us look at the significance of one of these images,
perhaps the most well known and widely used, the body of
Christ.

This image is used by Paul in an almost disconcerting
variety of ways. It relates the Risen Christ to both the Lord's
eucharistic presence and the community of believers. Christ
continues to be incarnate in his world through his Church.
It is a consequence of the Gospel, not an optional addition
to it. What are its implications? They are both ethical and
ecclesiological. Let me take a few examples from Paul's first
letter to the Corinthians. 'Do you not know that your bodies
are limbs and organs of Christ?' (1 Cor. 6:15). How then can
Christians abuse their bodies by fornication? That is the issue
with which Paul is dealing, and it is their incorporation into
Christ which is his clinching argument. We are not only
united with Christ in some sublimely mystical and metaphor-
ical sense. This is a physical expression of Christ's body about
which Paul is speaking.

Then comes the major eucharistic reference. 'When we

bless "the cup of blessing", is it not a means of sharing in the blood of Christ? When we break the bread, is it not a means of sharing in the body of Christ? Because there is one loaf, we, many as we are, are one body' (1 Cor. 10:16–17). This is more than fellowship of which Paul is speaking. The juxtaposition of these two references to Christ's body in the Eucharist and the one body of the Church leads us to conclude that our *identity* as well as community lies in Christ and in the unity of his body.

So we go on to the need to avoid division. A body torn apart dies. Already Paul has condemned the divisions in the Corinthian Church where believers were claiming allegiance to Cephas, Apollos, Paul himself or, the worst blasphemy, citing Christ as the leader of their faction. Then Paul used the image of a building to urge unity. Now when it comes to divisions within the eucharistic assembly he more naturally turns to the image of the body of Christ. 'He who eats and drinks unworthily eats and drinks judgement on himself if he does not discern the body' (1 Cor. 11:29). But we should not be tempted to think that Paul eschews judgement within the body. There is evidence in 1 Corinthians 5 that he believes there must be discipline within the body. However, he does not underestimate the way in which the body which exists to celebrate can be hurt in the exercise of judgement.

It becomes clear from his letter to the Colossians that Paul did not merely use the image of the body of Christ in relation to local Christian communities. In Colossians 1:16–18, he is talking about the whole Church of which Christ is the Head. This is the Church conceived across and between individual fellowships. The pre-existent Christ is also the Lord of the Church which is his body now.

> In him everything in Heaven and on earth was created, not only things visible but also the invisible orders of thrones, sovereignties, authorities and powers; the whole universe has been created through him and for him. He exists before everything, and all things are held together in him. He is, moreover, the head of the body, the church.

No evangelical doubts that Paul believed in the lordship of Christ over his Church but it is hard sometimes to distinguish

Christ from the Church in the language Paul employs. Is he using language sloppily? Are these epistles which became part of the canon of Scripture simply rushed letters hastily dictated late at night with no time to read over them in the morning? I think not.

The Church is not just a useful shorthand term for the community of the faithful. If it truly *is* the Body of Christ, the Church too demands our belief, trust and faith. John Muddiman expressed this in his book *The Bible: Fountain and Well of Truth*:[15]

> The Church is the place where belief is to be located, with the emphasis on the corporate and sacramental nature of faith; but also that belief can be directed towards the Church as its object.

Hence the credal formula, 'We believe in one, holy, catholic and apostolic Church.' That universal Church is not some myth removed from the reality of Christian believers; a nice idea which does not exist except in the dreams of ecumenical enthusiasts. No, the Church as the body of Christ is both a consequence of his incarnate presence in the world and anticipates the Church triumphant when angels and arch-angels and all the company of heaven will join in praise of the Father through the Son in the Spirit.

Despite all this, exploring the theological concept 'the Body of Christ' beyond what it might mean in relation to a local congregation has not been customarily a significant area of evangelical concern. Rather, evangelicals in the Church of England have traditionally given much more weight to the concept of a *national* Church. In some ways this is a legacy of the Reformation. However, this is not a specifically evangeli-cal ecclesiology. The concept of a national Church was strong amongst the Celts who resisted the authority of Rome, and the pre-Reformation struggles around the authority of the Papacy also had more than a hint of this kind of nationalism.

Although establishment continues, the concept of a 'national Church' is in practice declining in significance. As a result such evangelical thinking as there has been about the

15. Basil Blackwell 1983.

nature and doctrine of the Church has lost one of its chief pillars. There is therefore a good deal of instability around.

We see that in part at the local level and in particular in relation to ordinands. There is a significant number of ordinands in the evangelical tradition who have experienced conversion and spiritual nourishment outside the Church of England: in house churches, in independent evangelical fellowships, and still to some extent within the mainstream free churches. It used to be said of evangelical ordinands that their frequent response to questions about why they had chosen the Church of England in which to minister was 'It's the best boat to fish from'. This is not an adequate ecclesiology. It neither sees the Church as the ark of salvation, nor possessing a part in God's plan as any more than a comfortable institutional vehicle. The doctrine of the Church lies unconsidered.

In effect this leads to an even firmer belief in the primacy of the local congregation; defining this by its faithfulness to Scripture and the evidence of the works of the Holy Spirit within it. The Church as a broader and wider body becomes no more than a collection of such congregations. This, as it seemed to me, was the implicit assumption of John Tiller's report on the Church's ministry.[16] I sense too that this implicit assumption about the nature of the Church often surfaces in the General Synod. Some of the recent debates about episcopal discipline have suggested that some members of Synod, and not exclusively evangelicals, see the Church of England as an enlarged 'congregation' in which the bishops are defaulting 'vicars' or 'pastors'. But there is more to a traditional evangelical ecclesiology than this. Let me try to state briefly three principles within it which I discern.

First, the Church is affirmed practically. I do not think that Richard Baxter's *The Reformed Pastor*[17] is any longer widely read. But it still represents the ideal of church life and ministry. By contrast a tremendous number of biographies and 'success stories' are read nowadays by younger Christians. They assume that if the Spirit is at work within a group

16. John Tiller, *A Strategy for the Church's Ministry*, CIO Publishing, September 1983.
17. First published 1655.

of believers, there we have a church. It is a practical, as well as local, vision of church life; but Baxter is less a slave to the cult of success.

Secondly, the Church is defined by what it is not. This is part of the Reformation tradition and the reaction to papal authority which is enshrined in the Thirty-Nine Articles. It follows from my previous point. The local church, blessed by God's activity and presence, is wary of outside authority, whether pope, bishop or synod, lest this comes into conflict with the authority of Scripture and personal faith in Christ. This is no simple anti-papalism; it is equally anti-Presbyterian; though within the house church movement we see the development of some wider authorities, the most significant pope-like authorities within it are rooted within each individual community.

Thirdly, the Church is instinctively ecumenical. Evangelicals associated with like-minded believers in every tradition long before the contemporary ecumenical movement. In part this accounts for the early lack of involvement in that developing movement, which, together with a fear of compromise, meant that it was dominated by figures from the liberal and Catholic traditions. There is some justification in the evangelical claim *always* to have been ecumenical. But one of the problems of this, and of the lack of a developed, sustaining ecclesiology is that it is hard for many evangelicals to see what the problems are. My predecessor, Donald Coggan,[18] was sometimes accused of a lack of ecumenical tact in calling for inter-communion whilst in Rome. His instinctive ecumenism came from his evangelical formation. Now that all the churches seem to be emphasizing local ecumenism, the evangelical contribution to the ecumenical movement seems to be growing; but this is largely because this development fits in with traditional evangelical thinking.

Thus far I have stressed the way in which such evangelical ecclesiology as there is, stresses the local dimension of the body of Christ. Yet, you might say, do we not all live these days in a global village? Should we not cherish the local in an age of centralization in communications and even to some

18. Archbishop of Canterbury 1974–80.

extent in government? Whilst I firmly believe, along with G. K. Chesterton, that 'nothing is real unless it is local', the local loses its significance if not set within the context of the universal. That, surely, was one of the points Paul was making in exploring the image of the body of Christ.

The mobility of people these days might seem to lessen their sense of the local, but I am not sure that this is so. What it does do is make their associations temporary, including their sense of 'belonging'. In church terms this reinforces the idea of 'membership', but makes it temporary in relation to a local church rather than creating a sense of membership of the universal Church. There is, especially amongst evangelicals, but again not exclusively so, a very easy change of church affiliation these days according to where you happen to live. Perhaps too this is a product of that local ecumenism which we are encouraging. But the tendency is to look for a lively church, of whatever denomination or none, within striking distance of your home. The holding notion of 'parish' which Charles Simeon so firmly adhered to is lost, and with it the desire to ensure that there is a universal Christian ministry and witness, expressed through the parochial system, which ensures that the Gospel is heard, and those outside the Church ministered to. When we begin to create a doctrine of the Church which serves *only* our own spiritual needs, there are *grave spiritual dangers*; of spiritual self-satisfaction and self-centredness, a danger of creating the Church in our own image and letting, as St Paul says, one of the members rule the body.

I sense in a number of quarters a certain dis-ease with the predominance of the local in current evangelical thinking. In *Anvil*,[19] Peter Williams says 'Evangelicalism needs an ecclesiology which will make sense of the theological pluralism which actually exists because many people love and serve the Lord who are not evangelicals.' My belief is that evangelicals within the Church of England have a great deal to offer in this area. My desire is not to develop a narrow Anglican ecclesiology, justifying ourselves as a denomination over against the whole Catholic Church, but rather to develop an

19. Vol. 5, no. 3.

ecclesiology for God's Church. We do not claim as Anglicans
to be any more than *part* of the catholic and universal Church;
but we must *not* have a partial ecclesiology. Our doctrine of
the Church must be greater than ourselves. And the strength
that evangelicals bring is their spirituality and polity con-
tained within an episcopally ordered Church. As the world-
wide Church searches for an ecclesiology which can form the
basis of ecumenical agreement, the evangelical contribution
could be invaluable. Let me examine what those things might
be.

First, there has been a rediscovery of the *Church as Sacrament*,
expressed in the remarkable resurgence of liturgical scholarship and interest. Who would have guessed at the time of the
Prayer Book controversy in 1928 or in the 1950s that, come
the 1970s and 1980s, liturgy would be a major area of evangelical study, and that renewal in worship in the parishes
would be equally matched by scholarship which was reliable,
informed and yet innovative? What would the Church of
today be like without the Grove booklet,[20] the flagship of
Buchanan Enterprises! Not only is this area of study ecumenical in impact but it could also be usefully channelled as an
approach to the nature of the Church. Already we have Geoffrey Wainwright's[21] significant attempt at producing a system-
atic theology grounded in liturgy and worship. But much
more could be done.

The praise of God and the preaching of the Word are the
two key elements in the Church's liturgy, and any liturgy
worthy of the name seeks to combine local impact with universal significance. What the Church is doing locally in its
worship, it is not doing in a time capsule or in a geographical
vacuum. It is offering worship in union with Christians in
other ages, places and times. 'The voice of prayer is never
silent, nor dies the strain of praise away.'

Despite this liturgical renewal there is a tendency in some
quarters for a privatization, even trivialization, of liturgy.
Nothing is more dangerous than privatized religion and
nothing is more inimical to the evangelical spirit. For to

20. Books produced at St John's College, Nottingham, originally under the
    inspiration of Colin Buchanan, Bishop of Aston 1985–89.
21. Methodist theologian and liturgist; author of *Doxology*, Epworth 1980.

privatize religion is to possess it, and when we think we possess the Gospel then its saving power is null and void. And if we trivialize it we lose the sense of God's wonder, greatness and majesty.

The contribution of members of the Evangelical Alliance to liturgical renewal has been significant. It has reshaped the worship of the Church in many parishes, and it could become the basis for an ecclesiology which would bring evangelical insights about the Church and Gospel to bear much more widely. It would, you must remember, be a recovery of yet another great strength of the Evangelical Revival of two centuries ago. Charles Simeon once said, 'The finest sight short of heaven would be a whole congregation using the prayers of the liturgy in the spirit of them.'

The second strength of evangelicals is their belief in the *Church as signal to the world of the Word of God* and the way in which they take the Bible seriously. The Church cannot proclaim the Gospel to the world without the Scriptures. The Bible is the Church's book; not just the book of the local church but the Word which informs the whole Body of Christ and sustains it. The dangers of privatizing the Bible and domesticating it are apparent to Christians in every tradition. Unmistakably there has been a growth in evangelical biblical scholarship in recent years. Anthony Thisleton,[22] amongst others, has challenged evangelicals with the task of interpretation. Evangelicals, catholics, and liberals can all in their different ways give supreme authority to personal spiritual experience rather than to the Word of God. This leads to us using Scripture for our own ends rather than allowing the text to speak for itself. We must all continue to work hard at seeing what the writer of the biblical material is seeking to say in *his* context. Then the Scriptures are more accurately a Word from the Lord in our own situation.

For some people the product of biblical criticism has been a sterile faith; let us not dodge that; but this sterility as much arises from the primacy given to contemporary experience as from the use of critical principles. Walter Moberley's article

22. Of the department of Biblical Studies, Sheffield University.

Proclaiming Christ Crucified[23] is the sort of creative evangelical
use of Scripture which I hope will eventually get us away
from assuming there are such things as conservative scholarship, liberal scholarship, evangelical scholarship, catholic
scholarship. What we need to recognize is that these are not
forms of scholarship each vying with one another, but rather
there is one entity called *biblical scholarship* and everyone in
the Church has a contribution to make, for it is the Church's
own task.

The third area of strength *is in the Church as a society, a
fellowship of believers.* I have already commented upon increasing evangelical participation in local ecumenism and the high
value placed upon the local community of believers. The
Church of England as a whole in its local ecumenical outlook
has moved very much towards a traditional evangelical position of co-operation with other Christians on the ground. In
your tradition you have experience of some of the pains and
tensions in such associations in ministry, and these might
well form a contribution to that search for a wider ecclesiology, upon which ecumenical agreement might be based.

Then, fourthly, the notion of *the Church as Servant*, has been
recovered. It is a matter for comment in Michael Saward's
recent book that half of the Church Urban Fund trustees are
evangelicals, though he was quicker to notice this than I was!
Prominent in my Commission on Urban Priority Areas which
produced *Faith in the City*[24] were evangelical voices. This new
social concern has depth because of commitment to Scripture.
In this too you are rediscovering a tradition already apparent
in the Evangelical Revival. Shaftesbury[25] and William Wilber-
force[26] did not fight for the abolition of slavery on the grounds
of human rights for all, but because the slave was a brother
in Christ. Spiritual depth made the political campaign the
more telling.

Equally, in all that has sprung from *Faith in the City*, the
religious momentum comes largely from evangelicals linking

23. *Anvil*, vol. 5, no. 3.
24. See chapter 13.
25. Anthony Ashley Cooper, 7th Earl of Shaftesbury 1801–85; social
    reformer and factory legislator.
26. 1759–1833; philanthropist and advocate of abolition of the slave trade.

theology with worship, witness and social action. Whilst Anglo-Catholics have increasingly emphasized the need to maintain the churches as shrines, symbols of God's presence, and liberals have concentrated on criticism of the local authority, evangelicals have increasingly sought to combine social justice with a passionate insistence on Christian brotherhood based on the authority of Scripture and the experience of worship.

The evangelical movement and tradition within the Church of England has much to offer. Much of the vigour in our Church at the present time lies with this movement, and I give thanks for its faithful and imaginative witness to the Gospel. Evangelicals have strengths on which to build. They affirm, as I have tried to illustrate, the Church as Sacrament, as signal to the world, as society of believers, as servant of all. Here lies the basis for a doctrine of the Church which could be rich in theological significance and missionary endeavour. I hope and pray that this National Evangelical Anglican Celebration is not merely an expression of joy about the new and vigorous life in so many evangelical Anglican churches, but can look beyond its own tradition to see how the whole Catholic Church of Christ can equally be renewed and the Gospel more faithfully proclaimed to the glory of Our Lord Jesus Christ, the Saviour of the world and the Lord of the Church.

7

Sharing God's Gifts

The Archbishop's visit to Australia provided a welcome opportunity to strengthen the bonds that link the Church of England and the Anglican Church in Australia. In Perth he gave the sermon at a special Eucharist, attended by 8,000 people.[1]

The altar, to which the Archbishop refers, was specially made for the service. It was made up of four parts, which were divided at the end of the service, and transported to four new churches in North-West Australia where each part formed that church's new altar. The Archbishop preached later that week at the consecration services of each of those new churches in the 'outback'.

I set my bow in the clouds and it shall be a sign of the Covenant between me and the earth. (Gen. 9:13)

Even if there are not many clouds and only rare rainbows over Perth, there are many signs of covenant. You cannot make a covenant without partnership; and, happily, we can celebrate our partnership in the Gospel. Canterbury and Perth work *together*, and our worship is a sign of what we share.

The covenant which God made with his people enlarged their vision of the divine. And it is of an enlarged vision of what the Church should be in its mission that this Eucharist speaks. This very altar is a sign of that vision. Just as bread will be broken over it, so will this altar be broken up at the end of this service. Four altars for four new churches will be formed from it. They will be a gift from the Diocese of Perth

1. On 21 February 1988.

to the Diocese of North West Australia, to be used in four newly consecrated churches in that diocese.

This altar provides the theme for this address. Three things characterize it. It will be *broken*. It will be *shared*. It *unites*. And these three things characterize the Church in mission.

First, it will be *broken*.

There is pain in mission. We proclaim a crucified Lord, broken on the cross. Missionaries of every age and generation have had to face ridicule, indifference, persecution, martyrdom. It is reliably calculated that, numerically there have been more Christian martyrs in this century, the twentieth of the Christian era, that in all other previous centuries of that era put together. A world grown used to Christianity is not a world more tolerant of it.

Each of us knows some element of brokenness in our own lives. A failed marriage, a fractured relationship with one of our children, the loss of a job, a bereavement, a nervous breakdown. Which one of us has not known at some time what it is to be broken? Strong though humankind likes to appear, each of us is a strange mixture of strength and fragility. We are vulnerable, and the Gospel is 'Good News' because God has shared that vulnerability in Jesus Christ. He knows what it is to be broken. As our Epistle this morning reminded us 'Christ himself died to lead us to God'.

For Australian Anglicans engaged in mission, there is another sort of brokenness to be borne in mind as this altar is broken apart. All of us, if we are to grow into maturity, need to make some sort of break with childhood dependence on our parents. We love them no less through gaining our own independence. Rather we may love and respect them more. Parental wisdom can be drawn on more freely and, for some parents, their adult children become a source of mature advice. New, deeper relationships are formed. So it is with churches, in particular with the Anglican Church in Australia in relationship with the Church of England. Anglicanism and Englishness are not the same thing. You are discovering your own means of mission in this great country, a mission based on partnership within and between the Provinces of your own

Church. And in all this a new partnership between the Church of England and the Anglican Church in Australia emerges. It is a reflection of that mature relationship of parent and adult child I referred to earlier. The Australian church is now a source of mature advice for those of us engaged in the task of Christian mission in the 'First World'. Having made the break, your own integrity and vision as a Church leads to new possibilities in mission here and in relationship with those who hold the faith with you.

Perhaps though, above all, a broken altar reminds us of broken bread. The bread which is to be broken here is always bread to be *shared*. And this link between the breaking of bread and the sharing of it is crucial to our understanding of the Christian vision of God. Let us dwell for a moment on this *vision of God* which we have to *share*. A university chaplain in the United Kingdom once gathered a group of ardent believers from the student body together to discuss the priorities for Christians living in the university. He was taken aback by one young man who told him in a broad Scottish accent that his main purpose was 'to convince men of their vileness in the eyes of God'. What an astonishing view of Christian mission! Yet it has had enough currency to warp many people's image of the Gospel. How often people outside the Church do think that Christians want to make them feel guilty and inadequate. No wonder they get defensive and pour scorn on the Gospel. No, this is no way to evangelize; to imagine that you have to convince people of their wickedness before God can get a look in, is to ignore the enormous amount of goodness and love already present in non-religious humanity.

I believe better priorities in Christian mission are to encourage *thankfulness* and *reverence*. Let me digress to explain: these are close to the heart of what we have to *share* – and of which this shared altar is a sign.

It will always be true that some people come to faith as a result of suffering, pain or isolation. Very often we do see through the superficiality of our lives when faced by bereavement, a serious operation, a move to a new community, or

some similar life-changing event. The experience of knowing
our own fragility, of facing the possibility of being broken,
can lead to the search for faith. But the gift of faith can be
received at *any time* and we must not limit Christian mission
only to the times of crisis in our lives. What about those
reasonably responsible, humane and happy folk who seem to
get along quite well without God: how is the Church to engage
in mission to them?

I believe it is best done through engendering a spirit of
thankfulness, of gratitude. Many people who have little sense
of God somehow wish to say thank you; to whom, they do
not know, but the desire is strong none the less: Thank you
for falling in love; Thank you for the birth of a child; Thank
you for the strength I have somehow found to cope with that
bereavement. Everyday experiences of this sort can make our
hearts leap and desire to give thanks to someone or something
out there. Richard Harries, now the Bishop of Oxford, once
remarked that *either* we live our lives with a sense of resent-
ment or bitterness *or* we live with an underlying thankfulness
for all the new experiences, delights and opportunities each
day brings. That thankfulness is a path to faith, indeed a
kind of inarticulate faith in itself. It implies that life is good
and that it is God-given. And so all sorts of things can become
the occasion for gratitude, as G. K. Chesterton put it so well:

> You say grace before meals all right,
> But I say grace before the play and the opera,
> And grace before the concert and the pantomime,
> And grace before I open a book,
> And grace before sketching, painting, swimming, fencing,
>   boxing, walking, playing, dancing,
> And grace before I dip my pen in the ink.

Thankfulness – that is the theme of every post-communion
prayer and every new liturgy. 'We thank you for feeding us.'
Those of us who share broken bread become thankful to
God. And that spirit of thankfulness leads us to *revere* God.
Reverence follows thankfulness. 'Father, we offer ourselves to
you as a living sacrifice.'

It is because we are so lacking in reverence, in godly fear,
not just in the Church but in the world, that so many of our

problems arise. How can you cope with communities torn apart by racial bitterness or religious bigotry? How can you prevent the most sacred and intimate moments in human relations being trivialized into cheap sex? How can you prevent the polluting and destroying of our environment? Are not these, at root, questions of reverence?

The Church in mission proclaims the love and knowledge of God through Jesus Christ. Its authority to do so consists in cutting down the mighty in size, exhibiting itself in love and in patience, bearing the blame; that is the mission of a cross-centred faith. And such a mission invites the response of reverence. It invites us to see God at the heart of all things, willing us to respond to his love but never forcing us to do so.

Thankfulness and reverence: these are things we have to share. They are qualities often missing from life today because we have so largely lost our vision of God. But the vision of God, if we share it, inspires these things.

Though this altar is to be broken and shared, it also *unites*. It is not just the unity in Christ of those who break bread around it, important though that is. The altar also stands for the unity of humankind with God. Unless we see God as supremely valuable, we begin to miss the true value in everything else. Imagine what a world without any sense of God would be like. Every experience would have temporary significance. Eradicate the idea of God and even pleasures become joyless because death and decay would have the last word on everything.

Where bread is broken and shared, where there is thankfulness and reverence, a sense of God is engendered which unifies our experiences. Things begin to cohere, to drop into place. Where faith is present, the most ordinary pleasures become delights; even unavoidable suffering becomes somehow just bearable knowing that Christ has suffered too. And the people around us evoke in us a sense of thankfulness, even of awe and wonder. We feel at one with them and with God. Nothing is ordinary any more. The whole creation finds meaning and unity *in* God and *for* God. To experience that perfectly is the life of heaven. The Christian life is sustained by that vision and by the knowledge that it can be glimpsed and tasted here on earth; Christ has promised us that. He has given us this Eucharist, this simple meal, as a token of God's promise and covenant to his people.

And so this very altar reminds us of our priorities in Christian mission. Never be ashamed of your brokenness. Never be afraid to share your vision of God. Always praise him by thankfulness and reverence. And never forget that Jesus Christ frees and *unites*.

8

The Russian Millennium

In 988 the baptism of Prince Vladimir, Grand Duke of Kiev, took place shortly before his marriage to the sister of the Byzantine Emperor. His invitation to Greek clergy to evangelize his country opened the way to the spread of Christianity in Russia.

A thousand years later, that country celebrated not only this millennium but a new openness towards its people and towards religious practice.

The Archbishop joined around 600 international religious leaders, together with representatives from within the USSR for this event. Here he records his impressions – and reflections on Christian belief in the Soviet Union.[1]

In 1988, within a few days of each other, Moscow witnessed the visit of President Reagan, the public celebration of the Millennium of Christianity in Russian lands and a Party conference at which the Secretary of the Party not only openly practised *glasnost*[2] but also received at least a lip-service endorsement of the rather more difficult task of *perestroika*.[3] Only a few years ago none of these things would have happened in the way they have now. Moscow, though still technically a 'hardship-post' diplomatically, is now perhaps the most interesting place to be. However, the timing of my visit to Moscow was, in principle, dictated by a thousand years of history rather than politics.

I had been to Russia a good number of times before becom-

1. A talk given to the Great Britain–USSR Association in London on 11 October 1988.
2. Openness
3. Restructuring.

ing Archbishop of Canterbury. As Archbishop I was cautious about a visit to the Soviet Union. The Soviet Government has a certain skill at using official visits for its own purposes. And they are very well aware of the technical status of the Archbishop of Canterbury in the protocol of the British establishment. Just before my enthronement I became *persona non grata* by public criticism of the disappearance of human rights activists just prior to the Moscow Olympics. Overnight the large Russian delegation which was about to embark for Canterbury was down-graded and reduced to a mere archbishop and interpreter. But the archbishop who came said to me privately: 'Here are the presents of the others; they are here with their hearts.'

So July 1988 was not only appropriate historically, it was also right in other important ways. In the first place, the Millennium celebrations were far less susceptible to state interference than a so-called Christian peace conference. Secondly, I judged the Millennium celebrations the right occasion to show international Christian solidarity with Russian Christians who must look to a future as well as to a past. And, most obviously, we now witness the demand for radical change within Soviet society and in Soviet international relations from the leadership of the Party itself. It was the right time to go to Russia.

The Russian Orthodox Church also judged the occasion right to organize one of the biggest and most widely representative celebrations I have ever experienced. Almost four hundred international religious leaders converged in Moscow, together with over a hundred representatives from within the USSR, for a ten-day marathon of long liturgies, banquets and speeches. It was said to cost 1,000,000 roubles a day. But as a member of the Holy Synod said to me: 'Now is the time to make the most for the future by making the most of the past.' The Church had judged that the largest possible international gathering was the best investment for the future. I, for one, do not wish to be parsimonious about their judgement. Such a large celebration undoubtedly had its drawbacks. Russian organization can be eleventh hour at the best of times. It became clear that only the senior hierarchs really knew the detailed programme. And they were not staying with the international guests. So our accompanying Archimandrites and lesser bishops had the responsibility of getting their guests from hotel to cathedral or monastery or Kremlin without the benefit of an accurately time-tabled programme.

On the first evening we went to a vigil in the Epiphany Cathedral. I saw there a fascinating cameo of traditional Russian religious attitudes. Visiting ecumenical prelates were diverted to the south transept door, so great already was the press of the crowds. As I entered the cathedral a gipsy-like woman came in behind me and so gained a place next to the Iconostasis. She stood impassively during the elaborate ceremony and splendid singing. But on occasion she gently stroked the gilded icon screen; for her the holy was tangible. There was another woman at the Iconostasis, a black-swathed nun busily lighting and extinguishing candles. She saw me perspiring in my robes in the great heat and disappeared behind the screen to reappear with a glass of cold water. After this act of ecumenical mercy she suddenly turned on the other woman and tried to remove her from her sanctified position. But the first woman would not be removed, not for nun, deacon or archpriest. She clung to the holy. Here were Mary and Martha; the Mary, on this occasion being a Mary Magdalene. Both said something about Russian piety as if the revolution had never happened.

The heart of the celebration was in the Sobor, the Synod or Local Council of the Russian Orthodox Church. It took place at the Monastery of the Holy Trinity and St Sergius in Zagorsk, to which the guests went for the ceremonial opening and closure. The business sessions were restricted to the members of the Synod; though the membership not only included all the bishops and metropolitans but also elected clergy and laity as well. The laity, incidentally, achieved membership of the Russian Synod in 1917, half a century before the Church of England!

The Sobor looked to the past by canonizing a number of Russian saints, including the icon painter, Rublev. The list of saints did not include the martyrs of the twentieth century. And there was some grumbling even in front of the guests about this. I was thanked afterwards by a number of people for speaking of the Russian martyrs of the twentieth century in my congratulatory speech. The answer from the platform was interesting: 'We have now begun the process of canonization and, by implication, it would eventually include the martyrs of the 1920s and 1930s.' In spite of *glasnost* now, including public recognition of Stalinist terror, the Church had not yet got that far. I felt that on this and other issues the Russian Church has not yet quite abandoned the caution it has learnt in a hard school. This can be seen as an ecclesiastical example of the more general Soviet problem of inhibited middle-management.

At the ceremonial sessions of the Sobor, as if to reinforce this caution, next to Patriarch Pimen sat the Chairman of the Council for Religious Affairs. New freedoms there may be, but there had been false springs before. Nevertheless the Sobor did grasp the opportunity for the future by passing a new code of church statutes. We should not underestimate their significance, even though they have yet to be reciprocated in matching legislation on the part of the state.

Among the most significant of the new statutes is the restoration of the chairmanship of the local church council to the parish priest. This was taken away in 1971 when a layman appointed by the local soviet for church affairs was substituted. This was a device for isolating the priest and controlling the business of the parish. Another statute will allow the church at local level a limited ability to transact financial business. This was said explicitly to mean an eventual possibility of involvement in social projects. Priests may now also visit institutions such as hospitals – all prohibited before. The draft code had also laid down standing provision for the regular calling of a Sobor every ten years. This was successfully amended from the floor and the time halved to every five years on the grounds of the pace of change in the Soviet Union. Provision was also made for the retirement of the Patriarch, prompting speculation that the infirm and conservative Pimen might shortly retire.

A great deal will depend upon the corresponding state law. This has not yet been revealed, though it has been promised for later this year. When the chairman is in this country in November I shall be asking how this is proceeding. It is known that Archbishop Kyril's committee has had more than one important meeting with members of the Council for Religious Affairs. An interesting fact is that the Church feels able to debate its internal statutes in the open. No doubt it helps the Church to have had an international audience at the Sobor as witness to its aspiration.

Perhaps as important as the actual text of the Church statutes was this open debate at the Sobor; especially the business sessions which were duly reported by Russian friends. In 1971, during the Kruschev persecution of the Church, no one had departed so much as a word from the set text of their typescripts. But in 1988 there was debate and criticism. The most critical comments were made of the publishing department of the Moscow Patriarchate. Russian Bibles and catechetical literature were required, not Western language books which might give the reader innocent of history the impression that there had never been any difficulties between Church and State.

I had made a special request to go to Kiev. Though there were official celebrations in Kiev, these were after the Moscow events and formed part of a whole series of regional programmes. The baptism of Prince Vladimir (Woldomyr as the Ukrainians would insist) took place in the Dnieper at Kiev. Without accepting everything said on the Ukrainian side of this historical dispute with contemporary significance, I did want to record the historical fact by making a pilgrimage to Kiev.

Metropolitan Philaret of Kiev is second in the hierarchy of the Russian Orthodox Church, and is a loyal spokesman for it at many ecumenical gatherings. He is also, however, a Ukrainian. On the visit of the Foreign Secretary to Kiev earlier in the year, Metropolitan Philaret made it clear that he expected me to go to Kiev, and I had thought to have used my visit to Kiev to urge the restoration of the premier Russian holy site to the Church: the Lavra of the Caves. In fact the State announced that it proposed to do so during the Millennium celebrations, and I was able to be present in the Ukrainian Council for Religious Affairs as the chairman handed over the title deeds of the Monastery of the Caves to

Metropolitan Philaret. Predictably this was given publicity but I had not expected to be greeted afterwards by so many Russians saying they had seen me, and the handing-over ceremony, on nationwide Soviet television. Indeed Russians and guests alike were surprised at the extensive coverage of the Millennium each evening, including speeches, worship and prayer, but also some fascinating question sessions with young people.

The following day I was taken over the Lavra of the Caves, or rather that part of it which has been restored to the Church, which is indeed the most ancient and the most sacred to the Russian Orthodox. On that day in Kiev we not only saw the Lavra of the Caves but also informally visited both the working cathedral, where Ukrainian piety was deeply impressive, and the marvellous Byzantine cathedral, now a museum. Afterwards we went to the Convent of the Protecting Veil of the Holy Mother of God, where the remarkable Abbess had just covered the interior with extraordinary frescoes (in an apparently still living pre-Raphaelite style). She had achieved this artistic miracle by arbitarily closing the church and telling neither her bishop nor the local council for religious affairs. She knew how to get things done!

To complete our Kievan pilgrimage, we were then led down a steep path to the River Dnieper and the traditional site of the baptism of Prince Vladimir. The path was so precipitous and slippery that we all had to hang on to each other: two cassocked Archbishops, Orthodox and Anglican, their clerical staffs, and the unbelieving but amiable interpreter. At the supposed site we found the way to the river barred by a newly laid tramline, a ten-foot embankment, and a dual carriageway. The only way to see the Dnieper and the place of the baptism of Prince Vladimir was to march up the tramway – to the amazement of the driver and passengers of frequent trams.

On return to Moscow and Zagorsk, the Sobor was concluded with a moving memorial for the Russian soldiers who had died in Afghanistan. Monks and prelates, some of whom had fought in the Patriotic War against Hitler, were not ashamed of medals or moist eyes. Here was an illustration of the deep patriotism of the Russian Church and the spiritual soul of a people whose official philosophy is a Marxist materialism.

Deeply impressive and moving as the memorial was, it also focused my one major misgiving during the Millennium celebrations. Was the identification of the Orthodox Church and Russian culture too close? What of other Christian groups: Baptists, Latin and Eastern-Rite Catholics, Lutherans? And what of the Jews and Moslems? A bishop from West Germany said to me: 'I understand the Byzantine tradition of the Russian Church, but for us, since the Nazi era, this degree of patriotism is unthinkable.'

We spent a whole day at the Bolshoi listening to speeches of congratulation from outside and inside the Soviet Union. The speeches from the hierarchs made clear enough the Church's commitment to *perestroika*. But one ecumenical observer, and Indian Orthodox metropolitan who is well known as a frequent visitor to Moscow Peace Conferences, enlivened the proceedings by voicing the question some of us had been silently asking: 'Is it not now time for *perestroika* in the Church?' He received considerable applause from members of the Sobor as well as from guests.

We were back at the Bolshoi that evening for a concert. Secular choirs were heard singing sacred music and, for the first time, church choirs were allowed on stage. Russian patriotism concluded the evening with a spirited rendering of the Soviet version of the 1812 Overture, complete with the Marseillaise (the former Cardinal Archbishop of Marseilles was duly present) but (as usual in modern Russia) without the Tsarist national anthem.

For the past few days my staff and their Vatican opposite numbers had been conferring together and trying to discover what exactly was expected on the following day where the programme cryptically spoke of a visit to the Supreme Soviet. At the Bolshoi the two staffs finally cornered Metropolitan Philaret of Minsk who told them that the Cardinal Secretary of State and the Archbishop of Canterbury were expected to respond to Mr Gromyko. It was good to have some warning. As we entered the Kremlin the next morning Metropolitan

Philaret turned to the Patriarch of Romania, Cardinal Casa-
roli and myself and said: 'Mr Gromyko, he will speak first,
the Patriarch will speak for the Orthodox, the Cardinal for
the Roman Catholics and the Archbishop of Canterbury will
speak for the rest.'

Mr Gromyko delivered a classically long and ponderous
speech; he surprisingly said he would now take questions.
The Patriarch of Romania then delivered an extremely long
speech in order to convince us of the excellent relations
between the Russian and Romanian Churches. No contrasts
were drawn with the strained relationship between the two
states, recently illustrated by Mr Gorbachev's snub to President Ceausescu. Mr Gromyko said, quite rightly, 'I do not
think that is a question. If you can't think of any, I know of
some you may wish to ask.' He then went on to give both
questions and answers in the classical manner. All this left
the Cardinal and me little time for our pieces. The Pope's
representative abbreviated his speech but put a good question
or two. And I delivered mine, somewhat unsatisfactorily, over
lunch, but used the occasion to speak of the need for religious
freedom, for *all* believers.

Our morning at the Kremlin was not, however, without
some profit for I was able to have some conversation with
Mr Kharchev. I raised the particular case of a deacon in
prison and I also asked him who was responsible for St
Andrew's, Moscow, the former Anglican Church and long
since a recording studio. He said such a matter would indeed
come to his desk. There is discussion in Moscow among
expatriate groups about the restoration of this beautiful
church. It would not be an impossible task to restore it,
perhaps as an ecumenical centre.

The Moscow celebrations were now drawing to a close.
There was a final Sunday liturgy at the impressively restored
Danilov Monastery. But the worship was out of doors and
the weather cold. What is more, it was clear that those closest
to the sanctuary were not all of the faithful. It was apparently
a ticket only occasion and the front ranks were filled with
those who, as someone put it, 'can get tickets for the Bolshoi'.
It was interesting that they should have wanted to be there
at all. The believers were at the back and the final liturgy

was not charged with the potency of faith which had been so apparent at the opening.

This was also the time to listen to other voices. My staff made a visit, in private but not in secret, to a number of so-called Christian dissidents, including Father Gleb Yakunin and Alexander Ogorodnikov. I wondered whether I should meet them myself, but they understood why I could not easily have met them. This would have meant numerous accompanying hierarchs and what we wanted to know was what they really felt about the official Church. Such a conversation would have been inhibited and limited to courtesies.

The attitude of the dissidents towards the official Church displayed slight divisions amongst them; but they understood its passivity. This had been necessary for survival in the past. Yet the Church must now see that things are changing and it must grasp every opportunity. In particular the Church must have modern teaching material available for the many inquirers for adult baptism. Criticisms of the publishing department of the Patriarchate were even sharper than those of the Synod.

The new church statutes were seen by them as moving in the right direction, but the actual poverty of the Church was stressed in spite of the richness of the furnishings of its buildings. Above all, and this was interesting coming from a radical group, the Church needed to invest in centres of spirituality and holiness as beacons in a materialist society. This group said how handicapped the Church was by not being master of its own statistics. Not even the bishops really knew the size of the Church; only the bureaucrats in the State Council for Religious Affairs office. We had heard many facts and figures in the formal speeches, but it was a new revelation that their central register was *solely* in the hands of the State.

Gratitude was expressed for Western Christian interest in Christians in the Soviet Union, not least through Keston College,[4] All had been amazed to see Michael Bourdeaux[5] on Leningrad television only a few days after last-minute pressure to obtain an entry visa for him. As in all Eastern European

4. Research Centre specializing in the study of religious communities in the USSR and Eastern Europe.
5. Director since 1970 of Keston College, Keston, Kent.

countries, appreciation was also expressed for the external services of the BBC. They listened to my own Christmas message for the BBC Russian Service each year.

I believe these Millennium celebrations to have been a major land-mark in relations between Church and State in the Soviet Union. For the moment this mainly concerns the Russian Orthodox Church, though in private conversation with the Roman Catholic delegation, I know precise achievements were negotiated for both Latin-Rite Catholics and even the Ukrainian Catholics. Much now depends on how the State responds to the new confidence embodied in the new church statutes. It was said that Moscow itself had pressed for the restoration of the Lavra of the Caves in Kiev against the wishes of the local Soviet in Kiev.

Much will also depend on new leadership in the Church. We must pray that the opportunities will be grasped and we must work hard at exchanges and visits at all levels to encourage this to happen. At Zagorsk there was already a most important beginning of collaboration between the monastery librarian and the US Library of Congress.

We are now able to send theological college students to Russia seminaries; though I have to say the task of finding Russian speakers is made no easier by the run-down in Russian studies in this country. And we are expecting to receive a significant young theologian from Leningrad at one of our colleges. I believe it is by such mutual exchange that the Russian Church will be helped to grow in confidence.

Nor will such contacts only have ecclesiastical significance. An acquaintance of mine, who was once a Russian diplomat in London charged with keeping an eye on religious affairs, is passionate for real reform and, though still an unbeliever, arranged for me to be interviewed by *Pravda* of which he is literary editor. The first time a religious leader has been given such space; the text accurately reflected what I wanted to say about spiritual and human values.

It is not accidental that this new interest in religion comes from the intelligentsia. Any acquaintance with Russian literature past and present reveals the Russian writer and poet grappling with theological themes. The conclusion of a film now being seen in the Soviet Union has an old woman asking her way to the church in a village where the Church has long since been destroyed. That road used to lead to the church, she is told. 'What use', she asks, 'is a road without a church?'

Yet neither Church nor State yet knows how to respond to this. There *is* a new confidence in the Church, but it will require leaders of imagination and initiative to guide the Church into a freer society where it must enter a debate with both practical and theoretical materialism. Paradoxically, the qualities Mr Gorbachev most needs in his government departments and local soviets is also this quality of imagination and initiative. Post-revolutionary Russia has encouraged neither of these things in either Church or State.

Will the enforced inertia of so many years allow a new flowering of Russian religious life? How much will *perestroika* have really achieved if eventually it simply delivers consumer goods to Soviet shops? These are two separate questions in formal logic. And yet Mr Gorbachev often speaks of 'human' values, and it is clear he is thinking in the broadest cultural terms, which for the Russian must include religion. So perhaps my two questions are really one. And we in Britain need to be much more aware of the potent link between religion and the Russian soul if we are accurately to assess what is happening in the Soviet Union. According to the legend of St Vladimir, his motive in sending out emissaries in search of a new religion a millennium ago was in order to unite his kingdom. And the reply which came from those emissaries who visited Hagia Sophia in Constantinople was: 'We knew not whether we were in heaven or on earth.'

Of course, the whole process might be put into reverse and old ideologies again enforced, but my feeling is that things have already gone beyond the point where reversal would be easy; that much is clear. For the moment the Russian Orthodox Church has to be congratulated on its Millennium festivities, not only as a spiritual celebration but, above all, as the Church becoming *visible* again: and this in a deeply symbolic, iconographic, culture. The Church has also begun to put its house in order in terms of the rules by which it governs itself in relation to wider Soviet society. But like the Soviet

Government itself, it must now do more than pay lip-service to words. There are some leaders in the Church who are capable of grasping the new opportunities apparently beginning to be offered. I shall not only be with them in prayer but continuing my friendship with them, and my encouragement, in the crucial months and years ahead.

I will end with a story which gives hope while also illustrating the ambiguities. On the day I returned to this country the foundation of an entirely new church was laid in a Moscow suburb. Afterwards the chairman of the Council for Religious Affairs delivered a short speech in which the foundation stone was spoken of as the 'incarnation', and the technical theological term was used, 'of Leninist principles of religion'! I do not think any of the several people who reported this to me knew exactly what was meant. Probably he himself would not be easily able to explain it. But it looks to me like the beginning of revisionism on a grand scale, and I was profoundly glad to be present at the Millennium celebrations which were in part its catalyst.

SERVICE

9

Michael Ramsey

Lord Ramsey, 100th Archbishop of Canterbury, was much loved and respected for his scholarship and his spirituality. In this funeral address[1] Robert Runcie paid tribute to him.

Dying and behold we live (2 Cor. 6:9)

At the very heart of the New Testament there lies a movement from death to life, a struggle in which death and life are at odds with one another, and in which life is victorious. Our part, the part of every Christian, is to let our life and our death be drawn into the living and dying of Christ so that in him our deaths may not be dead ends but a way through and a beginning of life eternal.

Such thoughts may be ours at any funeral. They are particularly appropriate at the funeral of Michael Ramsey. He was a man who, alike in his life and teaching, spoke eloquently about the present reality of eternal life and yet clearly knew in all its sharpness the experience of dying with which our world is filled.

If we ask what was his outstanding characteristic we may say it was his sense of the reality and nearness of God. A sense that he conveyed by all that he was, as much as by all that he said. *An unselfconscious awareness of God.* It was that which we saw and loved in him. It was that which won the respect even of those who disagreed with him. It was that which drew the seeker and won the spontaneous affection of children and strangers. Some of us can recall how we felt it twenty-seven years ago in Canterbury Cathedral as he gave

1. At the service in Canterbury Cathedral, 4 May 1988.

out his enthronement text: 'There went with him a band of
men whose hearts God had touched' (1 Sam. 10:26). We
recall perhaps the lift of his voice, the lilt of the words themselves, the unforgettable refrain, the searching invitation:

> Help one another, serve one another, for the times are
> urgent, and the days are evil. Help one another, serve one
> another as from this hundredth ceremony at St Augustine's
> throne there goes a band whose hearts God has touched.

He has gone on ahead to join the great company of those
who have gone before. Sometimes he spoke of them as if of
intimate friends; of his beloved Anselm whose quiet unassum-
ing scholarship sprang out of the deep hidden life of prayer,
who yet won battles for truth and righteousness without the
weapons of worldly subtlety or strength. Part of the legacy of
his time in Durham and York was his love for the saints of
the north. He spoke of Bede who 'because he was a good
man, could live without shame and die without fear'.

Michael Ramsey was not someone living in the past or in
despair of the future; you had only to see him respond to the
eager student. Nor was he a remote figure, though often
graciously preoccupied. With his silent delight in responding
to the tourist photographers or in assisting a wheelchair up
the steps, despite his natural clumsiness, he endeared himself
to a whole family. His gift was serenity. Let us ask a portion
of it for ourselves, indeed for our English Church which he
loved and served so dearly. He reminded us where that serenity is grounded.

Pilgrimage was a favourite word coming for him out of St
John the Evangelist's description of the life of Christ on earth
as being all the way a journey to the Father. Now that he
has gone on ahead to where, in the phrase from St Augustine
he loved to quote, 'We shall rest and we shall see and we
shall love and we shall praise', it may be we can see more
clearly the heart of what he was saying and take it to
ourselves.

He was a great believer in silence. He was a great believer
in the illumination which love brings. In the quietness of our
affectionate remembrance of him, can we see the heart of it?

Towards heaven and towards the world's darkness. That

is how he described the journey of Jesus to the Father. The Church has a like journey in Christ's name, towards heaven in adoration and into the heart of the world in serving it. Christian pilgrimage as a single movement towards God in adoration and into the world in service was Michael Ramsey's deep perception. He spoke much of the glory of God, the glory of heaven, but he always insisted that was the glory of self-giving love revealed supremely on the cross.

There was no hint of ecclesiastical triumphalism about him. He taught the truths of faith with simplicity and conviction; but he was never contemptuous of another's religious faith. He took doubt seriously. He took the wounds of the world seriously.

By temperament a scholar and a contemplative, he did not fear to commit himself on practical questions of the day; on the rights of immigrants, on the death penalty, on our attitude to South Africa. The timeless quality of his vision shaped his perspective on them. It did not remove him from their urgency and demand.

Many have come to Canterbury out of respect for him whose name is inseparably linked with the search for Christian unity. From his student days he developed a sensitive and well-informed appreciation of the Orthodox. No Archbishop since Theodore of Tarsus has entered so deeply into the thought and vision of the Greek fathers. In return he is esteemed throughout the Orthodox world. His ecumenism was never that of one who waits for the world to become Anglican. His commitment at home to the scheme for unity with the Methodists was passionate; the longing of a convert from a Free Church childhood. His fortitude when it failed was an inspiration for the disappointed.

It was in relationships with Rome that the greatest changes took place in his time as Archbishop. His visit to Pope Paul VI established the theological dialogue whose achievements he has watched with joy and high hopes. On that April day, twenty-two years ago, he received from the Pope the episcopal ring he wore till his death.

When Michael preached the centenary sermon of the great

missionary, Bishop Frank Weston,[2] he ended his tribute by saying, 'It would displease him if we tried to be too solemn about him. So let the last word be that of the African boy who said, "You know he is a loving man for his mouth is always open ready for laughter, for he is laughing and will laugh for ever." ' Michael too would not wish us to be too solemn about him. He had a huge capacity to enjoy his ministry in spite of so many pressures and duties which must have been unwelcome to him. He found space for prayer, taking a retreat at Cuddesdon even whilst Archbishop and introducing silent croquet on the lawn. He found space for reading; when asked how he found time for his prodigious reading, he said 'I approach it like an alcoholic his drink, secretly and often'. He found space for people; he had a phenomenal pastoral memory, astounding me by his remembrance of the personalities of Liverpool in the days of my youth and his curacy. He found space for laughter; in this he was certainly shakeable.

No single person helped him to achieve all I have said more than Joan. As we owe her our sympathy at this moment, we owe her our gratitude. Although words cannot express the intimate depth of this happiest of marriages, our admiration for it cannot be unspoken, nor our prayers for her forgotten.

During his last weeks at a convent in Oxford, Michael would often cross the road to the little shop and post office where he bought his stamps and posted his letters. The young man who ran it, a Muslim from Bangladesh, enjoyed serving him and came to visit him when he was dying. During the conversation he asked Michael how long he had been ordained. 'Nearly sixty years,' Michael replied. 'Oh,' said the young man, 'that is a very long friendship.' Michael was thrilled. 'A very long friendship, a very long friendship', he loved the sound of it and smiled and in the nearer presence, we may surely trust, smiles still.

In a lifetime's service of God and the people of God, Michael Ramsey lived in such a way as to draw us all, of whatever allegiance we may be, a little closer into that friendship. The cost of receiving it is knowing that our journey is

2. Bishop of Zanzibar 1908–25.

the twofold one which is yet one and the same; towards heaven as we enter more deeply by Christ's own way into our true humanity. How *deeply* human a man in Christ we thank God for in Michael Ramsey.

10

All Saints Day

The great Christian feast of All Saints was the occasion of the following address. It was given, on 1st November 1988, at All Saints Church, Margaret Street, in London, a church which has played a significant role in the Anglo-Catholic movement.

> These are they who have put off mortal clothing and have put on the immortal and have confessed the name of God. (2 Esdras 2:45)

The nineteenth-century American writer, James Russell Lowell is now little read, but he used to be much quoted by Catholic preachers on All Saints Day. Though no Catholic himself, he once wrote:

> One feast, of holy days the crest
> I, though no churchman, loved to keep,
> All Saints – the unknown good that rest
> In God's still memory folded deep.

The poem, though, presents a problem. It assumes all the saints are dead and no more than a charming memory. The God in whom they abide is distant. Their memory is still. God's folds are deep. But we celebrate the Feast of All Saints because God *lives* and the saints have shown us that he lives in them and so may live in us. We give thanks also for this great Church of All Saints, and the living Gospel written down the years here in and through the lives of ordinary men and women, and being written still. Here has been focused with a rare continuity a tradition of spirituality both Anglican and Catholic. For countless men and women, All Saints

Church, Margaret Street, has been home, their spiritual home, where they have found God real in this life and caught a glimpse of the God who would be real for them forever. The saints of God join us who worship on earth with the worship of heaven. In the music of this Mass which can often express the unutterable because it does not have to pack its message into the capsules of ideas, in the still mystery of Christ's sacramental presence, we touch eternity.

But All Saints Day does not take us into a dream world. Holy people and holy places earth our piety by giving us a *sense of proportion* and the *perspective of hope*.

First, *proportion*. Every Christian age has had ecclesiastical problems. When we give them our undivided attention, we often find that we are trapped in them. Our very attention makes us absorbed in an ever-shrinking world. Synods have sometimes taken away my Lord, and I do not know where they have laid him. When that happens, we must cast our problems into a wider setting. So we shall hear something of the laughter of heaven; not cynical laughter, nor mocking laughter, but the laughter of triumph, the laughter of those who know that in the end 'all things shall be well, all manner of things well'.[1] Thomas More[2] went to the scaffold, in part the victim of ecclesiastical troubles. But before he died he comforted his old friend Thomas Pope, now divided from him in religion, by saying, 'Pray for me and I will pray for you and all your friends that we may merrily meet together in heaven.' Whatever the seriousness of the ecclesiastical conflicts of their day, More saw that, in the end, they would be together in the laughter of heaven. That Chelsea statue of him beside the Thames captures his steadfastness, but not the breath of heaven.

Father Stanton[3] had something of the same spirit. He once spoke to a group of ordinands and told them, 'When you are priests, tell your people to love the Lord Jesus. Don't tell them to be C. of E. Tell them to love the Lord Jesus.' The saints of God draw us away from institutional preoccupations and get us to look to Jesus. They belong to the whole Church.

1. Julian of Norwich (*c*.1342–*c*.1413), *Revelations of Divine Love*.
2. 1478–1535.
3. Arthur Henry Stanton, Curate of St Alban's, Holborn; died 1913.

Thank God we do not only revere those whose ecclesiastical loyalties fit our own.

A sense of proportion has often meant that holiness and humour have kissed each other. I remember worshipping in All Saints Church in 1945 on the evening of V J Day,[4] which was also the Feast of the Assumption. One might have pondered whether our victory in the Far East or the taking of Our Lady into heavenly glory would take precedence. Instead, I heard Cyril Tomkinson[5] begin his sermon with the words, 'Today is the birthday of Napoleon III.' A sense of proportion is a great gift. It prevents us giving eternal significance to transitory tensions. It punctures our pomposities. It means that worship and honour and glory and blessing and power are God's alone.

Then, secondly, this Feast gives us grounds for *endless hopefulness*. Those who shine in glory were once such strugglers as we now are. The saints lived in no golden ages. They too were stuck into ecclesiastical problems, often into debates of a ferocity which makes the heat of our little discussions seem chilly. The saints, let us remember, were frequently wrong in their political, or even theological opinions. What we remember about them is their fidelity to Jesus, not their points of view on the issues of the day. Who now agrees with the line that Keble, Newman and Pusey took over Irish disestablishment? Who, amongst those who value the Catholic movement in the Church of England, even remembers that this was the springboard for the renewal of Catholic tradition in our Church? More than ever, the Church of England needs this tradition. This is a tradition of sturdy optimism about human nature. If the image of God in humanity has been marred, it has not been destroyed. Here in All Saints Church, men and women have poured out their hearts to the Saviour in penitence and have received through the grace of absolution his forgiving and renewing love. We believe in the infinite possibilities of human nature because we know that to God all things are possible. The Anglo-Catholic movement, which All Saints Church stands for, was born not in despondency but

4. 15 August 1945, the day on which the defeat of Japan and the end of the Second World War was celebrated.
5. Vicar of All Saints 1943–51.

in hope. Yet one hundred and fifty years ago Anglo-Catholics were a real minority, far more of a minority than now.

Here in All Saints Church there are three things which need cherishing from the past and taking into the future. And, by taking them into the future, the optimism of the saints will be shared and the whole Church helped to glimpse that vision of God which is the life of heaven.

First, Butterfield[6] created a church which brings us to our knees. It was to be the setting for a liturgy which lifted the soul to God. In days when some are tempted to retreat into narrowly based, strident or do-it-yourself forms of worship, we need to cherish through our liturgy our communion with the Church through the centuries and throughout the world.

W. H. Auden in his play, *For the Time Being*,[7] devises a prayer for the contemporary worshipper of a comfortable, diminished God.

O God, put away justice and truth for we cannot understand and do not want them. Eternity would bore us dreadfully. Leave thy heavens and come to our earth of water clocks and hedges. Become our uncle. Look after baby.

Amuse grandfather. Escort Madam to the opera. Help Willy with his homework. Introduce Muriel to a handsome naval officer. Be interesting and weak like us and we will love you as we love ourselves.

Secondly, All Saints has maintained a long tradition of spiritual direction. I think of the hours which Kenneth Ross[8] spent as a confessor in this church. Unfashionable in the 1960s, spiritual direction has moved back to the centre of Christian life. There is pressure for more and better spiritual directors, more teaching on the spiritual life. Many seek it elsewhere, but catholic Anglicans have a tradition to draw on which is neither rigidly formal nor superficially matey. Catholic Anglicans should see that spiritual direction remains high on its internal agenda.

Then, thirdly, some of the most enduring theology and

6. William Butterfield, 1814–1900; architect of All Saints Church, Margaret Street, London.
7. Faber 1943.
8. Vicar of All Saints 1951–69.

poetry of faith in the Church of England during this last century has come from catholic Anglicans. I think of Kenneth Kirk's vision of God,[9] Austin Farrer[10] or Michael Ramsey, the poetry of T. S. Eliot or the drama of Dorothy Sayers.[11] All Saints Church is theirs. We need today a theology which is rooted within the Church and its tradition, takes contemporary thought seriously and lifts the imagination above sanctified sociology. I hope that the renewal of the Institute of Christian Studies here is a sign of your determination to make this church once again a centre for the study of a theology which inspires, has soul and converting power.

On this Festival of All Saints I pray that you will bring gifts we need into the Church we love – and can sometimes feel so anxious for. Among the memorable sermons preached from the pulpit at All Saints there is one by Neville Figgis.[12] Figgis, Mirfield father, confessor, scholar and encourager, was warning people not to be cast down by ecclesiastical difficulties or godless cynicism. He preached with a sense of proportion and sturdy optimism.

> The Church goes on. Its adversaries have pronounced it dead a thousand times – and cried to carry out the corpse for all was over bar the shouting – and they have even taken themselves to shouting, only to discover that the slain Hydra had put out another head and all was to do over again – for the Easter Hope is inexhaustible.

I pray for this confidence for all of us. Believe your calling: it *is* the living God who calls each and every one of us into the company of all the saints.

9. In his Bampton Lectures 1931; Bishop of Oxford 1937–54.
10. 1904–68; theologican; Warden of Keble College, Oxford, 1960–8.
11. 1893–1957; writer and theologian.
12. John Neville Figgis CR, 1866–1919.

11

St Dunstan

Ascension Day 1988 was the millennium of St Dunstan, Archbishop of Canterbury during the tenth century and one of the greatest of the English saints. A thousand years after his death Robert Runcie spoke in Canterbury Cathedral to a large congregation, many of whom regularly worshipped in churches dedicated to St Dunstan.

'The Lord has won a name by His marvellous deeds. He is gracious and merciful.' With these words from Psalm 111 on his lips Dunstan died in Canterbury. On May 17th 988, Ascension Day, he had preached three times in the cathedral. On May 19th he died. Today *we know* that the Lord has won a name by his marvellous deeds.

For twenty-eight years Dunstan was Archbishop of Canterbury,[1] one of the longest-serving occupants of the seat of St Augustine. It is a humbling experience to preach about so illustrious a predecessor. We have little that he wrote but a drawing of Christ survives, showing Dunstan as a small monk bowed low before him, a charming self-portrait. It is the Lord who has won a name through his marvellous acts. Dunstan is but his servant.

The age in which Dunstan lived was troubled. He was born just ten years after the death of Alfred the Great.[2] Gradually England was being rebuilt after the devastation of the Viking invasions in the previous century. Alfred's reign brought the beginnings of unity and peace. But society remained violent, lives were frequently cut short. Dunstan himself, in the course

1. 959–88.
2. *c.*849–99.

of his long life, lived through the reigns of no less than eight
kings. When so much of the good ordering of society depended
on the character and capability of the king, this made for
constant instability. In his youth Dunstan had been drawn
into the court of King Athelstan,[3] and his outstanding abilities
had been recognized. Dunstan might have been a career
statesman. But he chose the way of the monastic life and the
service of the Church. He possessed a remarkable clarity of
vision. He knew the country needed a steady spiritual heart-
beat, so his primary aim became the reform and renewal of
the monastic life. During the Viking invasions the earliest
monasteries of England had almost all been destroyed. Dunstan and those who worked with him set about the foundation
of new communities and the restoration of monastic life and
worship in churches which were in the hands of ill-organized
clergy.

It was a way that led to deeper spiritual life for the Church,
but in the tenth century this was not done in ecclesiastical
isolation. It was not a flight from the world, but was to
shape the character of the world. The monasteries, as here in
Canterbury or in Winchester, were often placed in the centre
of cities, the monks involved in all the life of the surrounding
society. They were not only places of constant prayer but
centres of Christian teaching, active welfare, of scholarship
and artistic achievement. His *Regularis Concordia*, or monastic
agreement, of 970, set out and codified the reforms in the
monastic life. It is a great work which, in its own words,
gathered customs, 'even as honey is gathered by bees from
all manner of wild flowers and collected into one hive'. Such
a method is characteristic of Dunstan, for he read widely,
prayed deeply and learned from the life of continental monasteries he visited. The Agreement is full of common sense
for monks. They should not chant prayers too quickly, nor
indistinctly; they should chant them at a pace and with a
diction which ensures that mind and voice agree, and, 'the
brethren shall not gad about visiting the properties of the
monastery' . . . unless absolutely necessary. St Augustine's,
Canterbury, was one of the monasteries reformed and rebuilt

3. King of Wessex 925–39.

by Dunstan. So it is most appropriate that we should process there after this service.

Another feature of the *Regularis Concordia* is the very special place given to intercessions for the King and the Royal Family. He drew up a coronation rite which is the direct ancestor of the service still used today in Westminster Abbey. In it the Church clearly recognizes the sacred, God-given character of the sovereign's authority; he becomes the Lord's anointed. But in it too the King recognizes his duty to uphold the law, to defend the Church, to punish wrong-doers, to temper justice with mercy and to care for the widows and the fatherless. The Anglo-Saxon Church, for all its limitations, had a deep sense of its duty to the whole of society. A duty symbolized by the growing use of the English language in teaching and preaching. Learning was not to remain a clerical preserve, shut in by the use of Latin. It was to leaven the whole life of society.

Dunstan died in peace, before those Viking raids which were to lead to the martyrdom of his fellow Canterbury saint, Alphege. Perhaps Dunstan's body is still near the High Altar in Canterbury Cathedral. Dunstan's body was certainly here in 1508 when a check was made in order to counter certain claims from the west country about the saint. There has always been a little rivalry over Dunstan between Glastonbury and Canterbury; although the rivalry must now be described as gentle, for it is I who have been asked to preach at Glastonbury for their great pilgrimage day dedicated to Dunstan on June 25th. And today we have a visible link with Glastonbury in the form of the pilgrims who have walked from there during the past five days to be with us here at Canterbury for this service, and joined with them there are many others from different parts of our world where Dunstan is honoured. Though he reformed the English Church, his name and memory lives on in the dedication of churches in places as far apart as the United States, New Guinea, South Africa, the Philippines and Malaysia.

Through the mists of history we catch glimpses of a very human figure. We know that as a young man he suffered from serious illnesses; illnesses which may have had psychological as well as physical causes. We know that he suffered temptations; for example the story of his catching the devil by the nose with red-hot tongs. Surely this suggests someone who has not without fierce temptations in dreams and fantasies. Like many great characters he had a complicated temperament. There must have been tensions between his longing for prayer and silence, his artistic gifts on the one hand, and his wider public and practical abilities on the other. He knew doubt and hesitation about becoming a bishop. We are told that he played his harp so well it was said to play itself. His singing was out of this world. Dunstan's love of craftmanship is legendary, especially his metalwork and casting of bells. Jewellers, bell ringers, goldsmiths and the ancient and honourable Goldsmiths Company have him as their patron saint.

It is little wonder that until the murder of St Thomas à Becket, this holy, canonized and very human character, St Dunstan, should have been the principal Canterbury saint and that so many churches represented here today bear his name. He was made a saint by acclamation and has been revered as such for a thousand years.

It may seem hard to answer the question, 'What can we learn from Dunstan?' We do not live in Anglo-Saxon England, and also it often seems harder to learn from towering greatness than from those more nearly like ourselves. Yet, in an age of specialization and fragmentation, we can admire and learn from someone who moved so easily in so many different fields.

Dunstan cannot have been a metalwork bore, for he had so many other talents. He cannot have been a religious bore, because of his broad interests and deep knowledge of the world. He cannot have been a political bore because policy to him was but a means to peace, justice, and godliness of life.

And so we could go on. For his life was marked not by finding a single track and staying on it, but rather by his service of God in a whole variety of interests and commitments; all was centred on his life of prayer and dedication to God. The dedicated man does not have fewer interests than others. He may well have more, but they do not disperse and disintegrate him for they are all held together by the central controlling movement of life, the movement of offering and praise and adoration and thanksgiving to God.

In the life of each one of us there are many different interests, different friends, different attractions, different temptations. Sometimes they can divide and dissipate. It was said of a character in a novel I once read, 'he was not so much a person, more a civil war'. It could never have been said of Dunstan. When all things come together to praise God, then we become not a bundle of parts but someone who can say, 'Praise the Lord, O my soul, and all that is within me bless his holy name'. Holiness and humanity, high office and humility – not always do these qualities go together, but in Dunstan they did; his life was all of a piece.

At the centre of each one of us there is that innermost heart, that place where all our thinking and all our dreaming, all our acting and all our willing, all our feeling and all our loving are rooted and grounded and brought together, a person made in the image of God. Dunstan, like all the saints, found that innermost heart was one that could respond to God with the whole of his being. The gifts God gave him were powerful but they did not pull him apart; because his heart was in the right place he could become what God wanted him to become. It is in the innermost heart of each one of us that we find Dunstan is not far away. Through his example we can draw nearer to God as he draws near to us in Canterbury Cathedral, the Church of Christ which Dunstan loved and adorned with his gifts and his presence. In our very different world we too can become what God wants us to become if our heart is in the right place. His marvellous acts have won him a name to be remembered and to God be the glory through Jesus Christ our Lord.

12

The God of Battles and the Fight for Faith

During the First World War British, Australian, New Zealand and other troops were landed at Gallipoli, Turkey. The campaign was a disaster, but the very scale of the massive casualties the Allies endured, and the heroism and courage that were displayed, have become legendary.

One of the chaplains at Gallipoli built a memorial chapel in his church – Holy Trinity, Eltham. An annual memorial service has been held there ever since, and since 1985 this has been complemented by a lecture reflecting on the lessons of Gallipoli. Previous lecturers include the Duke of Edinburgh. In April 1988 the Archbishop delivered this lecture.

The Aegean and the Black Sea are fairly well known to me as a classical scholar and Hellenic traveller. Many times I have sailed past Gallipoli and through the Dardanelles. I have experienced the chatter of a cruise ship conjuring up the ghosts of history and the drama of those waters; the stories and myths of Leander and Xerxes, in sight of the mound of Troy where Hector and Achilles fought and died. Then I have experienced the tribute of silence that descends as we have passed the memorial-marked peninsula of Gallipoli pointing almost accusingly like a finger into the tranquil Aegean hummocked with the isles of Greece; a silence prompted not least by the presence on board of veterans of the campaign itself.

I have some experience of war as a combatant. Gallipoli was the most ambitious, amphibious operation in the annals of history until the Normandy invasion. Those of us who fought in the Normandy campaign were aware of the preparations made for it and could not fail to be heartened by the thought that Winston Churchill – the daring architect of the 1915 adventure – was determined that close on thirty years later the mistakes would not be repeated. Perhaps those of us who survive owe a strange debt to the shadow of Gallipoli. Yet I am an archbishop and not a historian or a soldier. For that reason I can use Gallipoli as a back-cloth to 'the God of Battles and the Fight for Faith.'

> Go and may the God of battles
> You in his good guidance keep
> And if he in wisdom giveth
> Unto his beloved sleep
> I accept it nothing asking, save a little
> space to weep.

'I accept it, nothing asking . . .'. So wrote W. N. Hodgson,[1] the 21-year-old son of the Bishop of St Edmundsbury and Ipswich, in August 1914 at the onset of the Great War. The voice of Christian acceptance is here tinged with the patriotism of Kipling. His was but one of many voices which were silenced for ever in the ensuing conflict – in Hodgson's case, on the first day of the Battle of the Somme. Yet this verse may stand for the general sentiment about the Great War which long endured at home, despite the carnage at the Front. Not just Christian acceptance but positive encouragement to enlist and fight was the message heard from thousands of pulpits. Bishops, clergy of the Established Church and even Free Church ministers and leaders – many of them felt it their patriotic and Christian duty to assist the work of recruitment.

None was more enthusiastic than Bishop Winnington-Ingram, Bishop of London for the first thirty-nine years of this century. He declared his pride that there had been such an 'exodus of young men from church choirs, the Church Lads' Brigades, church Scouts troops and the ranks of the servers in response to 'an appeal to fight a duty to God as well as to the country'. Winnington-Ingram did not confine his activities to the men alone. He urged a rally of 2,000 women in October 1914 to say to their men, 'Go, and go with

1. 1893–1916; in *Verse and Prose in Peace and War*, 1916.

my love and blessing'. The Mothers' Union assisted the cause in the year the war began by producing a pamphlet entitled 'To British Women, How They Can Help Recruiting'. Alan Wilkinson's vivid account, *The Church of England and the First World War*[2] records the enthusiasm with which the Church generally greeted the war and the subsequent disillusion this ensured would be the consequence.

'Now God be thanked who has matched us with this hour.' The words are Rupert Brooke's,[3] as also the better known:

> If I should die, think only this of me
> That there's some corner of a foreign field
> That is forever England.[4]

Rupert Brooke's words like Hodgson's earlier were written before any experience of war. They are brave, patriotic words, often quoted by those who have never known the reality of war or forget the appalling and undignified suffering it creates. The glorification of war could not last at the front, and the questioning soon began. No doubt Rupert Brooke's style would have changed, had he survived. He died on the way to Gallipoli in 1915 of blood-poisoning following a mosquito bite.

Brooke would have been fortunate if he had survived Gallipoli, the carnage was so great. In part it is that carnage which occasions our remembrance. It would, however, be insensitive and superficial to omit any consideration of the strategy and tactics which dictated the Gallipoli campaign.[5] Even though I want to address the impact of war and the experience of war upon faith and the human spirit, I believe we should not neglect to recall what prompted a campaign such as Gallipoli. To attribute it to mere adventurism or to engage in easy denunciations of the military planners' disregard for the value of human life would be cynical and rash. I am suspicious of unconsidered, sweeping judgements. Human beings are more

2. SPCK 1978; Winnington-Ingram references at p.94 and p.36.
3. *Complete Poems of Rupert Brooke* (Sidgwick and Jackson 1939), p. 144: 'Peace'.
4. Ibid., p. 148: 'The Soldier'.
5. The landings of British, Australian and New Zealand troops in Spring 1915 and subsequent fierce fighting.

often mistaken than callous and my own experience of battle taught me how seriously strategies are considered and how protective officers are of the men in their charge.

Gallipoli was a campaign that failed. This has been its chief disadvantage in any subsequent assessment made of the motives which prompted it. It was hastily and badly organized. Intelligence was out of date. Maps were inaccurate and sparse. Communications primitive and chaotic. There were insufficient shells and few mosquito nets. There was bad security in Alexandria. The tactical objectives do not seem to have been co-ordinated into the overall strategic plan. The execution of the operation was flawed. Such is the general judgement. War in the Levant was not curtailed as a result and, if anything, the impasse on the Western Front was made the more politically intractable because of the Gallipoli failure.

There is no gainsaying much of this judgement. History is not made on what might have been but what actually happened. Yet Gallipoli was not a mad-cap adventure. It was part of a total vision of Churchill born out of the failure of the Navy to force the Dardenelles. There were good grounds for thinking that if we had broken through to Constantinople, where so much of the Turkish armaments industry was located, and Turkey was taken out of the war, a decisive blow would have been dealt to Germany from the rear. The precarious character of the Tsarist regime in Russia led to pessimistic assessments of that country's ability to maintain the war effort unless something was done to bring relief and assistance.

I refer to all this because I do not want us to be callously cavalier in judging the motives of military leaders when we think of the impact of the carnage of Gallipoli.

We should also consider the scale of Gallipoli in its romantic anticipation. To this place came an imperial army. The soldiers bore themselves, said John Masefield,[6] like kings in a pageant; their commander, the gentle and civilized Scot, Ian Hamilton, as he sailed to his battle station, wrote, 'The Aegean seems like a carpet of blue velvet stretched out for

6. From his short history of the campaign, *Gallipoli*, 1915.

Aphrodite'. The gifted young men of that generation in our countries seemed to be gathered together; future statesmen, writers, as well as amazing relationships; from W. G. Grace's son to the Australian journalist Keith Murdoch, who was to be such a thorn in the side of the British leadership and whose son Rupert has such a commanding influence upon the international news media of today. There were contingents of Sikhs, Punjabis, Gurkhas and the Ceylon Planters Rifles, also the Assyrian Jewish refugee militia, whose badge was the shield of David, whose orders were given in Hebrew and in English, and which was said to be the first Jewish military unit to go into action since the Fall of Jerusalem in AD 70. Above all they included the ANZACS, the Australian and New Zealand Army Corps. All this seemed to give a larger scale to the carnage which followed. It was Gallipoli and its quarter of a million Allied casualties which prepared the ground for the acceptance of war deaths on a hitherto unprecedented scale. The Somme and Passchendaele had this terrible precedent.

The scale of Gallipoli, the romantic dreams, the losses, the suffering, the extraordinary conditions the men met with had its own special impact on those who survived. It was, it seemed, more searing than Flanders for those who returned there and more memorable than Egypt for those who fought thereafter in the Near East. Most of all the intensity of the experience was felt by the ANZACs. This was the blooding of the Australian and New Zealand nations, just as Vimy Ridge was for Canadians. I have been privileged to speak both in Australia and in New Zealand at the dawn service on ANZAC day and have seldom been so moved by what was clearly an act of national recollection and religious dedication. A campaign like this created that sense of identity and solidarity essential to national pride. The conviction that war on such a scale must have a meaning on the same grand scale has been doggedly clung to by many. There was at Gallipoli a certain nobility of the human spirit, but to strain that out we need to look searchingly at the underside of the story.

For those on the beaches and in the trenches the depths of degradation and misery were soon reached. A. P. Herbert in retrospect captured in verse something of the nature of Gallipoli which makes the word 'blooding' appropriate not just for the ANZACs but for all who took part.

> This is the Fourth of June
> Think not I never dream
> The noise of that infernal noon,
> The stretchers' endless stream,
> The tales of triumph won,
> The night that found them lies,
> The wounded wailing in the sun,
> The dead, the dust, the flies.
>
> The flies! Oh God, the flies
> That soiled the sacred dead.
> To see them swarm from dead men's eyes
> And share the soldiers' bread!
> Nor think I now forget
> The filth and stench of war,
> The corpses on the parapet,
> The maggots in the floor.

What was true of Gallipoli was reflected elsewhere in the experience of war. A cause in which millions died must be potent with symbols of Good fighting Evil. Or so the soldiers were told. How else could these sacrifices and sufferings make sense? Though that remained an orthodox conviction at home it gradually grew less and less convincing at the Front. And even patriots faltered. Kipling, usually so stirringly patriotic in tone, began, after the death of his only son at Loos in 1915 to question his conscience.

> If any question why we died
> Tell them, because our fathers lied.[7]

There can be no doubt that, to many who fought, the world seemed to have gone mad. Yet from the theatre of war, particularly the First World War, springs some of the most enduring poetry in the English language.

In many cases it seems to have been *forced* from the minds of authors by the unspeakable experiences of trench warfare.

7. From the poem 'Common Form' from 'Epitaphs of War', *The Years Between* (Methuen 1919) p. 141.

Theirs were often minds which never, in the normal course, thought to express themselves in verse. Now they stuttered and exploded into unconventional and, to some, crude and unacceptable 'poetry'. The sentimental outpourings, inspired by the *idea* of combat, were all gone, leaving spirits raw and exposed. A compulsion was driving many frustrated soldiers to *words*, not to eloquent stirring verses, but to 'staccatoed, frantic expression of the truth' that was facing them.

One of the best, arguably *the* best, of the poets to materialize during this time was Wilfred Owen.[8] He was not new to the expression of life in words but had led a fairly sheltered and sedate existence before 1914. Owen was only one of many writers and chroniclers of the war years who felt moved to express the truth as he saw it in words, no matter how horrific the end product looked in black and white.

This process of expiation by composition was already well under way at Gallipoli. Two of the most vivid contemporary accounts were written by chaplains. Oswin Creighton, son of Mandell Creighton, Winnington Ingram's predecessor as Bishop of London, wrote *With the 29th Division in Gallipoli*. And W. H. Price, another chaplain, set down his reflections in *With the Fleet in the Dardanelles*.

The Revd Henry Hall, who established the Gallipoli Memorial Chapel here in Holy Trinity Church, Eltham, was also a chaplain in the campaign. He wrote to his wife: 'The landing was awful – men and officers shot down in shoals, caught in the wires, killed, wounded and drowned.' The desire to share something of that experience was deep but Hall's words are an inadequate expression of the horror. Whilst others resorted to poetry as their only means of stammering out fractions of the truth, Hall gave expression to his remembrance in the chapel here, another form of eloquent testimony and one in which God's share was assumed and unspoken. Hall was invalided out and returned to his parish not long after the campaign ended. Many of the chaplains at Gallipoli however, like the other men, did not survive to keep remembrance.

The war soon shattered facile notions of providential purpose. Victorian and Edwardian fantasies about 'Progress'

8. 1893–1918.

were also devastated. A sense grew up that there was an element of divine judgement in all this. That sense led the Church of England into organizing in mid-war the ill-fated National Mission of Repentance and Hope. But the War did not lead to the religious revival which some observers, then as now, always thought they glimpsed. Rather, at home, stories of German atrocities were increasingly accepted uncritically and this had a negative impact on the country's spiritual health. Responsibility for the war fell on Germany alone. She became its sole cause. The war effort was directed at ridding the world of Prussianism, this incarnation of evil. The Rector of St Anne's, Soho,[9] said: 'We are fighting not so much for the honour of the country, as for the honour of God. Not only is this a Holy War, it is the holiest war that has ever been waged.'

It was remarkable that humour sometimes laced the cynicism of the war poets. Siegfried Sassoon[10] was the most capable of combining the two, as in this extract from 'To any Dead Officer':

> Goodbye, old lad! Remember me to God,
> And tell Him that our Politicians swear
> They won't give in till Prussian Rule's been trod
> Under the heel of England . . .

Sassoon and others felt increasingly the division between those fighting in the trenches and those in England, unaware of the unmeetable demands patriotism was making on their fellow countrymen.

But you did not have to be a pacifist to possess a conscience and a faith strained to breaking point. It was sometimes the breaking of faith which seemed to allow some men to retain their conscience. Jackson Page, who died only in April last year, was the son of a Methodist manse who had been taught in a Methodist school. But, upon enlisting, there was a searing question which his faith could not answer: 'Can anyone ask

9. Basil G. Bourchier, 1881–1934; army chaplain 1915–16; quoted in Alan Wilkinson, *The Church of England and the First World War* (SPCK 1978), p. 254.
10. 1886–1967; from *Collected Poems*, Faber and Faber 1961.

Jesus Christ to help them fire a machine gun?'[11] He concluded that only a negative answer was possible and proceeded to remove Jesus Christ from his mind and consciousness. For him the experience of war removed his belief, a belief held from childhood, that God is Love.

Yet Jackson Page, despite a shattered faith, was deeply moved by the work of the chaplains in the war and felt that justice had never been done to their heroism. Some fell victim to cynicism. One chaplain though made a noted breakthrough to many men not only through the heroism of his ministry but also through poetry. Geoffrey Studdert Kennedy,[12] known affectionately as Woodbine Willie, was probably the best known chaplain of the First World War. Only Tubby Clayton,[13] the founder of Toc H, achieved a similar degree of fame as a household name. Kennedy's own ministry amongst the men was extended in scope by his excursions into poetry. His verse was rough-hewn. Much of it was intended for the men themselves. His dialect poems, published as *Rough Rhymes*, achieved popularity not because they were good verse – they were not – but because they addressed the dilemmas the men felt deeply but which were too awesome for them to express in words.

Studdert Kennedy knew the feeling experienced by the men. Not merely distance separated them from their loved ones. In his rhyme 'What's the Good?'[14] Kennedy has a soldier pondering what he has done to his so-called enemies who remind him even of his own son at home.

> There's a young 'un like our Richard,
> And I bashed 'is 'ead in two,
> And there's that ole grey-'aired geezer
> Which I stuck 'is belly through.
> Gawd, you women, wives, and mothers,
> It's such waste of all your pain!

11. Private correspondence quoted in Alan Wilkinson, *Dissent or Conform?* (SCM Press 1986), p. 55.
12. 1883–1929; army chaplain 1915–1919.
13. 1885–1972; Philip Thomas Byard (Tubby) Clayton, army chaplain 1915–19.
14. 'Rough Rhymes of a Padre' in G. S. Kennedy, *The Unutterable Beauty*, Hodder and Stoughton 1927 (new edn Mowbray 1983).

> If you knowed what I'd been doin',
> Could yer kiss me still, my Jane?
>
> When I sets dahn to tell yer
> What it means to scrap and fight,
> Could I tell ye true and honest,
> Make ye see this bleedin' sight?
> No, I couldn't and I wouldn't,
> It would turn your 'air all grey;
> Women suffers 'ell to bear us
> And we suffers 'ell to slay.

Wilfred Owen found outlets for this spiritual dilemma in the compassion of his poetry which was often focused on the enemy with whom he was in combat. His conscience was haunted by the enemy, as in his poem 'Strange Meeting',[15] found among his papers after his death from machine-gun fire in November 1918. It represents a kind of poetic nightmare in which the dead Owen is united with his enemy:

> 'Strange friend', I said, 'Here is no cause to mourn.'
> 'None,' said the other, 'save the undone years,
> The hopelessness. Whatever hope is yours,
> Was my life also; . . .

But British poets did not have a monopoly on conscience, as this extract from 'Requiem for the Dead of Europe' by a German, Yvan Goll,[16] shows:

> Before sticking your bayonet into his groin did not one
> of you see the Christ-like look of his opponent?
> Did not one of you notice that the man
> over there had a kingly heart full of love?'

These were the profound questions of war. The search after its purpose eluded many of the fighters, but many turned to God for answers, for hope and, often, in angry despair.

God was, indeed, on trial. Where did this degradation of mankind fit into God's purpose? How did those who poured

15. *The Collected Poems of Wilfred Owen* (ed. Edmund Blunden), Hogarth Press, 1931.
16. Pseudonym of Isaac Lang, 1891–1950 (translated from German); in *The Penguin Book of First World War Poetry* (Allen Lane 1979), p. 231.

their inner beings into words come to terms with it all? For many there *was* no justification. God had deserted them. Yet Owen, writing again to his mother, makes an interesting revelation from his experience. This was written in February 1918 (the year he died). Harold and Colin are his brothers.

> If I do not read hymns, if Harold marks no Bible, nor Colin sees no life-guide in his Prayer Book, it is no bad sign. I have heard cadences of harps not audible to Sankey, but which were strung by God: and played by mysteries to him and I was permitted to hear them.
>
> There is a point where prayer is indistinguishable from blasphemy. There is also a point where blasphemy is indistinguishable from prayer.[17]

Somehow it was a particular gift of Studdert Kennedy's to see this point which Owen expresses so forcefully. The horror, death and devastation, a blasphemy against the image of God in man, paradoxically drew men into God's presence. The crucifixion became a controlling image for the religious feelings of those who felt themselves being crucified. Studdert Kennedy's theology was shaped by this experience. He could only believe in a God who suffered with the men. It was not enough that Jesus suffered and died on the cross at a moment in history, and not even enough that the act should be of timeless significance. He believed all this, but God could only be God at the Front if he suffered *now*.

Studdert Kennedy was in revolt against an idea that God could only be experienced in serene and sublime detachment from his world. He satirized it in his poem 'A Sermon':[18]

> Seek not to know the plans of God,
> But pray upon your knees
> That you may love with all your heart,
> With all your soul and mind,
> This perfect God you cannot know,
> Whose face you cannot find.
> You have no notion what He's like,
> You cannot know His Will,

17. Harold Owen and John Bell (ed), *Collected Letters* (OUP 1967), p. 534.
18. *The Unutterable Beauty*, Hodder and Stoughton, 1927.

He's wrapped in darkest mystery,
But you must love Him still.

This is but part of a long poem consisting of a sustained caricature of sublime religion. It ends with a typical Studdert Kennedy refrain centering all upon the cross.

O, by Thy Cross and Passion, Lord
By broken hearts that part
For comfort and for love of Thee
Deliver us from cant.'

And it is the cross which made, for Studdert Kennedy, a nonsense of the unknowable, transcendent God, of the beyond. His theology knew no system but a great deal of pain. He could only express it in verse and in sermons because these were interpretations of life's experience.

The more enduring war poetry from men like Owen and Sassoon is sometimes criticized as unrepresentative of the soldiers' feelings. It is, of course, the mark of a great poet to perceive in the present moment significance which normally only future reflection might reveal. We should not be surprised therefore if poets are also prophets, without honour among their colleagues and kinfolk. But Studdert Kennedy did not suffer from neglect during his time. His work was intended for an immediate audience; he was on the soldiers' level, and he did communicate this sense of God mixed up in the senselessness of war.

Back in England preachers continued to describe the war as a fight for God, country and religion. Studdert Kennedy, and many other chaplains, soon ceased to believe that simple verity. They might not doubt the rightness of the cause; most could be as patriotic as the sternest anti-Prussian zealot; but it was the facile assumption that this was a fight *for* God and religion which could not survive the carnage. Gradually Studdert Kennedy came to believe that the soldiers were entering into God's nature in this conflict, a nature revealed most fully in the cross. For a religion which proclaimed a crucified Lord might be peculiarly able to cope with revealing divinity even in horror and bloodshed.

Robert Graves'[19] poem 'Recalling War' suggests that there was much anguished God-directed thought, even amongst those who could scarcely be described as devout.

> Even there was a use again for God –
> A word of rage in lack of meat, wine, fire,
> In ache of wounds beyond all surgeoning.

Perhaps this was so, that such depths and abysses were the prerequisites of a new and further spiritual understanding.

Even in the bitterness there seemed to be faith. The language of faith seemed inescapable whether in anger or in mockery.

> For fourteen hours yesterday I was at work – teaching Christ to lift His cross by numbers, and how to adjust His crown . . . I attended His supper to see that they should be worthy of the nails . . . with maps I made him familiar with the topography of Golgotha.

That was Wilfred Owen.[20]

I have juxtaposed here the idealism and the adventure of war so frequently expressed by those who are distant from its realities, with the heart-rending anguish of those who experienced its devastating effect on the human spirit of the combatants.

The Roman poet Horace fled from the battle of Philippi, and war never entered his life or his poetry again. English poets who fought at Gallipoli and in two wars created some of the finest poetry in our language. It may lack the harmony and facility of a Horace but it has the dimension of depth. Among them were those who ceased to believe that war could be the will of the Christian God. Yet they seem convinced that if he exists he never deserts us but works through the predicaments created by our history, our ambitions, and even our mistakes.

The time has come to attempt some concluding reflections. I state them succinctly but I hope not too obscurely. Professor

19. 1895–1985; in Robert Graves, *Collected Poems*, Cassell 1939.
20. In a letter to Osbert Sitwell written in July 1918.

Sir Michael Howard[21] has expressed clearly the moral dilemma which war must create in the human mind.

> Wars do not come simply from militarism and muddle. They may come, and indeed usually have come, from a deliberate intention on the one side to use armed force as an instrument of state and on the other a determination to resist it . . . The hard fact is that wars are caused as much by our virtues, our sense of justice, our belief in the difference between right and wrong, our loyalties, our readiness to defend a way of life.

That is why I cannot myself accept the pacifist option. Yet I believe that wars should only be fought with a pain in the mind. That is why I have no hesitation in supporting my friends in the Forces and in recruiting chaplains to serve them. It should be remembered that it is not the military who create wars. Indeed the activities of our Forces today are palpably deployed in attempts to prevent wars rather than to win them. Christ was kind to soldiers. The people he was tough with included the clergy as well as the politicians and publicity seekers of the day. To soldiers he was unfailingly sympathetic.

Furthermore, loyalty to a regiment, a ship or a squadron, like loyalty to a country, is a natural human feeling. Jesus the Jew wept in affection over his native Jerusalem, thereby consecrating such natural feelings and loyalties. Patriotism is *not* enough but it is a kind of nursery for loyalties which need to be deepened as well as extended in scope.

The Second World War, in which I fought, was surrounded by far fewer romantic dreams than the First and was not merely the product of thoughtless patriotism. We had learned something from the 1914–18 war but not enough; there is no time to explore this now, but simply to state baldly my own belief that war is always the result of failure, even if the last war had a sense of inevitability about it. It was a final resort.

I like the verses of Cecil Day Lewis, reflecting his own attitude to the Second World War.

---

21. Regius Professor of Modern History, Oxford University 1980–89.

It is the logic of our times
No subject for immortal verse –
That we who lived by honest dreams
Defend the bad against the worse.[22]

If it produced no heroic poetry, many of my friends died in it. I do not believe that they died in vain and I do not believe they would think so either. A war which closed down Belsen and Buchenwald was worth fighting.

Personally I find it difficult to believe in the God of battles, the miracle of Dunkirk, the angel of Mons. For me faith is not believing impossible things. It is trusting that the promises of Christ never fail. It is not hoping the worst will not happen, but believing there is no human tragedy which cannot be redeemed, that is, turned to good effect to increase the total output of goodness in th world. In Shakespeare's great war play *Henry V* the King says:

There is some soul of goodness in things evil,
Would men observingly distil it out.[23]

War is an evil, messy business, but even shared anguish can be a bridge of understanding and ultimate reconciliation. When I attempted to preach on this subject at the service following the Falklands Islands Campaign my subsequent correspondence revealed that it was not the combatants but the commentators who wanted to hear more about the God of battles and less about the fight for faith.

My favourite Gallipoli story is sentimental, but why not? On April 25th, 1965, the fiftieth anniversary, a group of veterans from Australia and New Zealand landed in small boats on the original bridge-head. This time they fell into the arms of Turkish veterans who had been their enemies. Their welcoming embraces were laced with laughter and with tears.

Some words from William Blake[24] to close:

Man is made for Joy and Woe;
And when this we rightly know,

22. From 'Where are the War Poets?', C. Day Lewis, *Collected Poems 1954* (Jonathan Cape, n.e. 1970), p. 228.
23. Henry V, Act 4, scene 1.
24. 1757–1827; from 'Auguries of Innocence.'

Thro' the World we safely go.
Joy and Woe are woven fine
A clothing for the soul divine.

13

Hope for our Cities

The Church Urban Fund was set up in 1988 following the Archbishop of Canterbury's Commission on Urban Priority Areas, to raise money for church-sponsored projects helping to reinvigorate the life of the inner cities and outer estates. This sermon was given at a service inaugurating the Fund, held at Westminster Abbey in April 1988.

Any great cause calls for a motto, a badge or an emblem. Jesus Christ is Lord. That is our motto. These words are the oxygen of Christian worship. They are the *fundamental* reason why we are gathered together in Westminster Abbey – from Coventry and Cornwall, Tyneside and Merseyside, Kent and Cumbria. Not simply for entertainment, though there will be some of that quality in it; nor for a political rally, though we have political opinions; nor for a social outing. The point of this gathering is that *the Lord is here, his Spirit is with us.*

The following parable comes from my own experience of a very different church from this. It was on an 'overspill' housing estate, grey and monochrome. The morning was cloudy and drizzly. As I approached the little undistinguished church my heart sank. Yet once inside I found such reverence and enthusiasm in the congregation that my spirits were raised as the singing nearly lifted the roof. We were making new Christians by baptism that morning. One of the adults was so thrilled that she embraced me and knocked off my mitre. The barriers were down, we were members one of another. After the service they followed a regular Sunday custom. They provided dinner for anyone on that estate who might otherwise eat it alone. We sat down, more guests than hosts, and I felt 'here is the Body of Christ'. He is Lord of all and not just of the Church and our worship had within it the imperative to meet human need.

Jesus was a regular worshipper; he went to his local synagogue. It was at such a gathering that his neighbours first heard his message, a message of hope for all who saw themselves as poor, captive or oppressed. It challenged the comfortable and complacent. It judged the present and promised the future. That message of hope and judgement was to be worked out with crowds and individuals, on hillside and in homestead, street and temple, through the mysteries of cross and tomb, but it was first proclaimed at the heart of a community at worship. They hung on his words, though the message disturbed them because it called for a response.

All these are reasons why it is appropriate that the Church Urban Fund, with its message of challenge and hope, should be launched here in Westminster Abbey. Every diocese is represented here. If the hope and promise of the Church Urban Fund is to be realized, it will need the co-operation of us *all*, for it is now widely recognized in Church and State that the problems of the inner city are not just the problems of the inner city alone.

The report, *Faith in the City*,[1] described some of the hurt and hope which are to be found in the cities and the housing estates of our land. It did not please everyone. It may not have got *everything* right, but it often takes honest disturbance to prompt us to resolute action. Since its publication there has been much activity in Church and State, but stories of hurt are still painfully told. Mother Teresa has reminded us of the plight of the homeless here in one of the world's wealthiest cities.

An Archbishop of Canterbury has links with two places, Canterbury itself and Lambeth. They are very different communities. Frequently I move between the two. To travel to Canterbury we drive through south London where blight of landscape is writ large; crowds of people, thundering traffic, elegant buildings next to the housing estates reminiscent more of military barracks than homes, barricaded shops with graf-

---

1. 'A Call for Action by Church and Nation', Report of the Archbishop of Canterbury's Commission on Urban Priority Areas, Church House Publishing 1985.

fiti on the boards; a sense of emptiness and suspicion seems often to brood there. Who created all this? We did. It is no good blaming the Government, or the social planners, or the local authority, or the architects. To find a scapegoat does not solve problems. Such urban waste dents people's faith; faith not only in themselves but in God. We want to reverse the sense of unloveliness which is always characteristic of the unloved.

The *people* of the inner cities give us plenty of ground for hope. Under the landscape I pass through and in similar parts of so many cities, such as my own native Liverpool, there are people who keep faith and hope and love alive. They put the rest of us to shame by their neighbourliness and cheerfulness. Many of them are here and we have heard the songs of one such parish. They belong to us and we to them. We must keep faith with them and draw strength from them.

We do not need to go more than a mile or two from Westminster Abbey to come across signs of the vision which may emerge from the heart of a worshipping community. There is a drop-in centre just round the corner in Vauxhall which is becoming a real centre of community for the elderly and those unable to find work. There is a family centre in Paddington serving mothers and children who are condemned to spending often up to a couple of years in bed and breakfast hotels with nowhere for the children to play during the day.

But we are not simply into ambulance work. I know many other places from Newcastle to Leeds, to Walsall to Tower Hamlets, where the Church is working alongside those who bring fresh employment and enterprise. Sometimes the Church can be the catalyst of a sense of belonging together. In our buildings are found doctors' clinics, training centres, workshops for the handicapped.

Many initiatives are abroad from government and financier, business man and architect, police and social worker, doctor and educationalist, landscape artist and civil engineer; all bringing God's justice in very practical areas of life; all showing compassion as a strength and not a weakness; all healing wounds of powerlessness; all enabling our brothers and sisters to work out their own solutions and put them into practice.

But, no matter how great the physical and material improvements of the inner cities, the underlying question is one of morale. The Church may seem a small and seldom advertised presence. Yet if Christians and other faiths can work together in trust, if they know they are supported by their comrades throughout the nation, they can achieve miracles for morale and local pride. Communities like individuals only prosper if they are loved. When Jesus the Jew wept over his native Jerusalem he consecrated our local loyalties.

I remember meeting a churchwarden beside a beautifully kept church in Salford. In the midst of towering office blocks and shopping centres it was an oasis of calm with some unemployed youngsters creating a rose garden around it. 'I don't want to be told', said the churchwarden, 'that I belong to an Urban Priority Area; I belong to Salford and the folk around here are as good as anyone in the world. It is a good place is Salford.' I liked that.

Faith is there; what we need are the resources. It is our hope that the Church Urban Fund will provide the seed bed to generate the support which our churches in every Urban Priority Area so urgently need. There is no shortage of claims upon us, some of which we are already trying to meet.

Frequently – and you may have heard of this – we have had calls for the Church to give a firm lead. Even I have heard them in my ivory tower at Lambeth Palace. On this matter the lead of your archbishops is unequivocal. We will keep faith with 'Faith in the City'. In partnership with others we shall help to heal a wound which threatens the strength of our nation. I want the Government, the whole Church, the whole nation, to know that the Church intends to play its part in the renewal of our Urban Priority Areas.

The millions of pounds that are needed sound a tall order. There are many other claims on our resources but if we fail this cause it will be a failure of nerve, a failure in imagination. We want to do things with people, not for them. We want to demonstrate that the use of our money is a test not only of our faith, but of our fellowship, one with another. We want to show that the comfortable *can* express solidarity with the uncomfortable.

The Government has declared its priority of effort for the inner cities. If we sometimes seem to criticize them, they should not be able to reply, 'Physician, heal thyself'. Business people see the point. They will help and are already helping, and many of them who have already shown the colour of their money are with us today. The Church Commissioners[2] will help and go on helping for a long time. Voluntary bodies will help and are helping us as never before. We are in partnership with other great charities. So now I charge you. Go back to your parishes and dioceses and say that we are committed to the Church Urban Fund. The story is told of St Francis that when he sent his Friars out to the villages and cities of his world he told them, 'Preach the Gospel everywhere. Use words if necessary.' I have had to use words. But it is by what we do and what we are that we shall be judged. Do we really believe our motto? Jesus Christ is Lord of *all*.

2. Church Commissioners: A joint Church and State body responsible for the distribution and management of the inherited endowments of the Church of England. In effect it is responsible for the stipends of the bishops and clergy of the Church of England.

14

A Pilgrimage to Glastonbury

At Glastonbury Abbey the Archbishop addressed the thousands of Angli-
cans who gather there each year for a pilgrimage on the last Saturday
in June. This Glastonbury pilgrimage had a special significance in
1988, the millennium of St Dunstan, once Abbot of Glastonbury as
well as Archbishop of Canterbury.

Jesus said, 'I am the Good Shepherd.' (John 10:11)

I am delighted to share in this magnificent celebration in
honour of the Good Shepherd and of his servant, Dunstan.
The Good Shepherd, you may remember, is one who goes
miles over the hills. This humble under-shepherd has come
miles over the lovely, gentle hills of England to be with you.

I link Canterbury with Glastonbury; two places sacred to
Dunstan, surely one of the greatest of the under-shepherds to
sit on the throne of St Augustine. Dunstan was a pilgrim who
belongs to Europe as well as to England; but his roots
remained here. Here he had studied as boy. Here he had
trained for the monastic life. Here he had holy visions, dreams
and temptations. Here, like many others who come to Glastonbury, he became aware of unity between the beauty of
holiness and the holiness of beauty.

A story is told that Dunstan had a fever and got a stick to
protect himself from imaginary mad dogs he thought were
chasing him. In his delirium he climbed on to the roof of the
old wooden church of St Mary and was found on the next
morning still there but peacefully asleep. The moral he drew
was of humble trust in God. Or, to use the language of the

Gospel, he discovered that it is the Good Shepherd who protects us from the wolves.

Dunstan knew the divine and the demonic. The world of spirits seemed all around him. But he was not a man in turmoil, a wild character as we might say. Experiences never mastered him; he was the master of his experiences. Why? Because he was God's servant and his consistent conviction was that the Church of his time should recover its spiritual roots; he wanted it to live transparently *for God*, to be the channel of his activity in the world. This gave direction, purpose and shape to his life and ministry.

When Dunstan was appointed Abbot of Glastonbury he rebuilt the monastery. He did so in two ways. The buildings were restored, but so too was the round of prayer, worship, study and work. The reformed rule of Glastonbury was soon to become the rule for all Benedictine houses. *For it was to the religious life that Dunstan looked to reform the Church's life, and to the Church he looked to unite the nation's life.*

I do not believe this is a story of antiquity. The religious life is no anachronistic irrelevance. When I was in Russia I was present at a most significant event, the handing back to the Church of its first monastery, the Holy Cave of Kiev (with ninety monks ready to move in). Monasteries and pilgrimages to them are part of the soul of the Russian people. In the renewal of youthful Christianity in Europe is any name so esteemed as Taizé? So, in our own Church, let us cherish the religious life and the new initiatives that spring from it. I think of the sick and dying children cared for by the All Saints' Sisters at Helen House; of the Franciscan Hermitage built patiently over a dozen years at Shepherd's Law; of the new mixed Benedictine Community beginning at Burford. The size of these enterprises is not significant; it is the prayer, service and vision of God they generate which sustains and nourishes the life of the Church more than we can ever know. We need religious communities. We need Christians who will pursue this vocation. We need to call people to it, to encourage those committed within it, to remind ourselves of the radical demands of the Gospel.

Of course it is not for us all. But though not for everyone, the religious life as represented by Dunstan and the others I

have mentioned is a sign to our fractured lives and fragmented
world of the place where peace and harmony lie. These lie in
God – in total self-offering to him.

Obedience – that, I think, is the most testing of the vows a
religious makes. Christian obedience is not a matter of keeping on the right side of God's law and avoiding his punish-
ments; it is about *acceptance* and *surrender* – God's acceptance
of us and our surrender in love and service to him. In an age
in which we increasingly seek to gain control of our own lives,
a surrender is unfashionable. But that inner surrender is the
only way to prevent things taking possession of us, the only
way to true freedom.

There was in Dunstan an inner harmony which came from
his surrender to God in prayer and service. The Church now
faces so many controversies that threaten to cleave us down
the middle that we do well to attend to Dunstan's own witness. There is a unity which can only be given to us by God
and not created or concocted by our schemes and desires. It
will be given to us through the life of prayer, the inspiration
of the saints, and keeping our eyes fixed on the heavenly
vision. That is how it was in Russia, where I experienced
something of the way in which the Church was kept alive in
days of persecution and compromise. And then, recently, I
was in Bedford, celebrating the life and ministry of John
Bunyan, who gave up all Catholic practices, even bell-ringing,
but kept and enhanced the practice of pilgrimage. Bunyan,
Dunstan and the unknown saints who have kept the faith
alive in Russia, in each of them there has been this consistency
of conviction and surrender to God in love and obedience to
the heavenly vision. On their own, convictions can be hard
and unyielding. What gave grace and beauty to Dunstan's
life was *the vision of God, of the heavenly kingdom.*

Dunstan's vision of God was accompanied by visions and
dreams. These can sometimes deceive. Though ours is an age
suspicious of visions, strangely we live at a time when fantasy
and sheer dottiness can often deceive the seeker. Someone
once proposed this test to know if a vision was true. If your
inward sight of another world makes this world seem of no
importance; if what you see is so dazzling and luminous that
it puts all your ordinary life in shadow; if the vision makes a

lovely landscape or the ring on your finger or a ladybird's wing look dull or tawdry – then it is false.

A true vision of God would never throw this world into shadow. It would make the world stand out with a brighter clarity so that we might begin to see reflected off the divine a subtlety and delicacy in the texture of the ladybird's wing that we never saw before. The vision of God never diminishes the glory of his creation; it always enhances it. That is why those with a vision of God seem so strangely at home in a world so seemingly torn apart by sin and selfishness. They see themselves surrounded instead by God's grace, beauty and love. Have you ever felt dismal or despondent in the presence of a holy man or woman?

Dunstan was an artist: an artist in human relations, an artist in music, an artist in metal work; he loved bells – the bells that ring out with joy in Bunyan's celestial city. He was blessed with talents that enable us to hail him as a creator of our nation as well as a church reformer. But he never grew conceited, for he saw himself always *in relation with God*. We have little that Dunstan wrote – mainly a few corrections to the work of careless scribes. However, we do have one drawing of Christ with Dunstan as a humble monk, drawn small in the corner. And there, written in Dunstan's own hand are the words, 'I ask you, merciful Christ, watch over me, Dunstan.' He would give no encouragement to those who turn their back in despair on the world. He gives no encouragement to those who would improve the world by ingenuity alone.

We come on pilgrimage to Glastonbury, drawn to adore God in this holy place in the Blessed Sacrament. So let us leave this place, refreshed by the history that is here, by the atmosphere of a holy place, by the example of a holy man in our own history and by the unchanging character of all Christian pilgrimage, to love God and save the world.

HEALING

15

True Healing

A centre for healing and counselling was opened in the autumn of 1988 in the crypt of the Church of St Marylebone – the parish church of Harley Street and the Royal Academy of Music in London.

The Archbishop dedicated this centre, and also the new organ recently installed in the church.[1]

> To shame the wise, God has chosen what the world counts folly, and to shame what is strong, God has chosen what the world counts weakness. (1 Cor. 1:27)

St Paul was fond of paradox. It was just as well. From the beginning the Christian religion presented a paradox to the world. Healing and reconciliation with God came through a crucified Lord. Suffering was not eliminated but redeemed.

This imaginative Centre for Healing and Counselling also has its paradoxes. A crypt for the dead to be entombed has become a centre for the living to grow in health. And I suspect that some who thought this venture folly when first conceived now see wisdom in it. It is one of those initiatives which shows just how much fresh energy is created when the Church acts in co-operation with other bodies and does not simply live to itself.

There is a growing respect among many people for what is often called 'alternative medicine'. It has been the Church's temptation to regard its own healing ministry in that category. Here you have broken through such restricted thinking. 'Alternative medicine' becomes 'complementary medicine'. The Church's healing ministry and the day-to-day work of a

1. On 12 October 1988.

National Health Service general practice are combined, not just physically in the same building, but held in mutual regard. At least I hope so. Proximity does not guarantee mutuality. This centre must be more than a medical super-market. But I do believe that to come to a Church centre to see a doctor and then to encounter people practising music therapy or to find others praying quietly in the chapel or simply finding space and time to talk helps us to see healing not simply as a technique.

Across the range of activities here two principles should, I believe, be firmly held. The first is *reverence for life*. Some time ago I was attending a discussion between doctors, lawyers and theologians. The subject was transplant surgery. One of the surgeons present had just put a kidney taken from a boy in Vienna into someone here in London. Then he said, 'I could not do this work if I thought I was simply dealing with a bundle of parts. I find it difficult to define life and I am not very religious. But what I have of faith teaches me to respect – no, more – *reverence* every person with whom I have to do.'

This sense of reverence makes human relationships possible where technology and technique are liable to create distance between surgeon and patient, between counsellor and client, even between priest and penitent. To put yourself in the hands of someone who seems to have a knowledge and expert-ise which far surpasses your own can be a diminishing experi-ence. Where people feel helpless, even when in the hands of the greatest medical expertise, they begin to lose the power to heal themselves.

So to my second principle. It was well expressed by Dr Patrick Pietroni of the NHS surgery here. He said, 'We have forgotten that man's spirit is the fundamental ingredient of his well-being.'

Let me tell you the story of another surgeon, this time an eye surgeon in the United States. He once described the case of a woman patient. A week after surgery he examined her and noted satisfactorily that all the tissues were exactly as he had left them at the end of the operation. Yet ten days later her original condition was beginning to return. At that point he sat down with her and said, 'I'm afraid you are under a misapprehension. I am a surgeon but not a healer. I put tissues together so that they can heal as they could not if they were separated. I cannot heal you. I can merely put your eye back together. Now I must do so again, because your eye has come apart again. But if there is to be healing, it will have to be yours not mine.' The patient was delighted with this frank personal relationship. A second operation took place and this time the original condition did not return. What the surgeon had done was to build on his reverence for that woman's life and establish a relationship with her which made her feel competent to manage her own healing. This, I hope and pray, is the vision which will inspire you here. *Reverence for life* and *encouraging people to be agents of their own healing* – these are twin principles to cherish and affirm.

But what is Christian about all this? The Church's ministry of healing consists, for the most part, in Christians recognizing that God's creative love is at work in and through the skill and service of many doctors, surgeons, nurses and other practitioners who may never recognize him. The difference lies in the fact that the Christian relates everything that happens to the struggle of God's love against the power of evil – a struggle focused in the life of Christ. The Christian sees the healing of disease as a reflection of the victory which Jesus has won. Disease is a sign of a disordered world. In the ministry of Jesus the cure of disease is but one aspect of the Lord's victory over everything that spoils God's creation.

We are often put to shame by the goodness, integrity and sheer lovableness of our non-Christian friends. But our task is to name the name of Christ, to carry about with us a sense of indebtedness, to offer daily the sacrifice of praise and thanksgiving. These things create in themselves healing and salvation.

I do, though, have one word of warning. It would be understandable, and excusable, if you thought that you had cracked the problem of how to treat the sick. But suffering and disease are not merely problems to be solved. Remember my text: 'God has chosen what the world counts weakness.' There is a sense in which human beings need their problems, and need them more than solutions. How we handle the disorders of life shapes the development of our humanity.

It was expected when the National Health Service came into being that the demands upon it would gradually wither away as society became healthier. Technological advance has partly ensured that the demands upon it are greater than ever. But this is not the only reason. What we are beginning to realize is that *how* a person's sickness is taken away from them matters. The elimination of one problem might only create another, if the symptom has been treated and the underlying cause remains. Many of us recognize how much disease and accident is the fruit of loneliness, anxiety, self-hate and antagonism, but few break out of a system that limits the role of medics and clerics to the cure of the symptoms of these ills. Here, I hope, a beginning is being made. Let us remember, that Job never found an answer to the problem of unmerited suffering. The problem remained insoluble, but *in it* he met God.

Sometimes people are bearing the sickness of others, or the sickness of their society like the Suffering Servant in Isaiah. We who follow the way of the cross must ask whether someone who is bearing another's burden might be realizing their true humanity, and whether to eliminate all their disease, straighten out all their tensions and discharge them without a care in the world, would be to diminish them rather than to make them whole. *This is not merely an issue for the medical profession. It applies equally to the Church and its ministers.* True healing comes *not* from eliminating problems but living through them, transcending and triumphing over them.

The Church of St Marylebone and all who minister in it deserve love and support. This is a church which might live on its status and its past. Instead this church has chosen to create something different. For 'to shame the wise, God has chosen what the world counts folly, and to shame what is strong God has chosen what the world counts weakness'.

16

The Gift of Easter

Traditionally, the Archbishop gives the Easter address in his own cathedral, in Canterbury. Here he spoke of the hopes that the resurrection brings.

> Blessed be the God and Father of our Lord Jesus Christ who, according to his abundant mercy, has begotten us again unto a living hope through the resurrection of Jesus Christ from the dead. (1 Pet. 1:3)

I can think of no other words of Scripture which express so confidently, so concisely and so comprehensively the meaning of Easter. From whom does Easter come? Easter comes from God because he is abundantly merciful. Through whom does Easter come? Through Christ by means of his resurrection from the dead. And to whom does Easter come? Easter comes to us all to implant in us *a living hope*. And all this is expressed in that brief text, and not just as a statement of fact but as a great song of thanksgiving.

The gift of Easter comes to us from God's abundant mercy. We think of mercy too narrowly if we think of it as God's forgiveness or remission of punishment for sin. God's mercy is needed and yearned for by those who suffer as well as those who sin, by the bewildered and heart-broken as well as the wayward and stubborn, by the poor and the lonely in their sorrow as well as the proud and arrogant in their guilt. The gift of Easter is the gift of the merciful God to *all* who recognize their need for mercy. It is as universal in its range as the gift of Christmas.

The Church needs to take care that it remembers this *universal* message of Easter. Christ's resurrection is not good news only for communicants and the committed. It is the power of God and the mercy of God *for us all*. Often much more effort is made in our parishes to draw the uncommitted and enquiring into Church at Christmas than is ever attempted at Easter. Where are the Easter equivalents of crib services, carol services, Christingles? Let us do more to ensure that we proclaim that Easter is for *all* and not settle for a humanistic interpretation of Christianity which suggests that the most God did for us was to become man. The most he did for us was to raise Jesus Christ from the dead. 'Why have all our troubles come upon our world?' said Solzhenitzyn[1] in the first sentence of a memorable lecture, 'It is because we have forgotten God.'

The gift of Easter comes through Jesus Christ by his resurrection from the death of the cross. His was a dark death; as dark in the cruelty and hatred which attended it as are the deaths of those at the hands of present-day terrorists; as dark in the seeming defeat and failure of goodness as any death that has ever been. The world showed then that the goodness of Jesus was out of place in it. The world tried to remove his goodness, to kill it and obliterate his memory. But God raised Jesus up. Man proposes but God disposes.

Christians must never forget that it was when Jesus Christ was at his weakest, when death had overcome him, that God triumphed and broke through with resurrection power. Too often we seemed to have lost our faith in the God who is able to work through suffering, through human weakness and through the pain that is part of the price of conflict.

In forgetting all this we direct our attention to ourselves and think that we might be able to bring about the Kingdom of God on earth by our own strength and efforts. So much has been written and said recently about the Church and the modern world, but in so little of it is any notice taken of what the resurrection means to us. We are weak, say some, because

1. Alexandr Isayevich Solzhenitzyn 1918- ; Russian dissident author and thinker.

our numbers are small. We are strong, say others, because we are sure our opinions are right. We shall succeed, say others, provided our policies are popular.

But the Church is a body which sees its purpose beyond its visible performance: that is why Christians have never given up their efforts to make the world a better place, however strong the opposition, however restricted their activity, however broken and scattered their work. St Paul said to the Corinthians, 'If I must needs glory, I will glory in the things which concern my weakness' (2 Cor. 12:9). The hope which comes from God lies beyond human optimism.

Easter is the majestic sign that it is God who rules in the kingdoms of men and women, and so all our programmes and strategies, or priorities and verdicts, are at best fragile and tentative. Of course we must order our affairs as honestly and as thoughtfully as we can; we must uphold moral standards; we must struggle for peace and justice; but alas for that man or woman who supposes that he or she has the last word on anything or that their verdict is final. Easter defies human vanity.

The gift of Easter comes to us as a living hope. Hope is not optimism. We use the word hope so easily and often it only means that we have planned something and are keeping our fingers crossed that it might turn out all right, whether it is the possibility of reconciliation in Northern Ireland or the Middle East or some more personal possibility in our own individual lives. Optimism and pessimism are often simply matters of temperament. Easter hope is much more radical and has much deeper roots. Its roots lie in that majestic Easter sign, a sign that nothing, not even the horror and darkness of Good Friday is beyond the capacity or the will of God to retrieve, to redeem and to transform into the seed bed of goodness.

That Easter hope is one our world needs. Television screens bring the intractable problems of our world into our homes; problems to which we see no end, for which we see no solution and which make us the more hope*less*. Many of us know illness or depression and the fear and the weakness which accompany it. But we know too that sense of miracle when health returns or there is peace after pain. Sometimes it seems impossible to escape the belief that the joy and happiness spring out of that darkness and pain. We gain from ordinary experience a faint glimpse of the power of the Easter hope.

The merciful God who has given us Easter has given us grounds for hope which are as firm, as unfathomable and as unlimited as is God himself. God's time-scale is not ours; his methods are not ours; his wisdom is beyond ours. But in raising Jesus Christ from the dead he has given us a sign which we can understand. He has validated and vindicated the goodness of Jesus. He has *in*validated those who rejected the goodness of Jesus. He has validated the gentle, accepting way of Jesus Christ and *in*validated the powerful motives of the self-seeking and the hatred and aggression which mustered to destroy Jesus and which is still so distressingly prominent in our world. God has validated the things that draw humanity together and invalidated the things which tear it apart. 'I, if I be lifted up,' says Jesus, 'will draw all men to myself' (John 12:32).

In January I was in Northern Ireland at a gathering of young people who had been assembled from every part of the world: from Africa and from Cuba, from the Lebanon and from New Zealand. They brought with them fears about Ireland and anxieties about their own safety; they were uncertain about what they would find. They knew of Ireland's troubles; indeed, most of them knew only of its tragedies. But they found their image of Ireland cracked and broken open like the Easter tomb as they met Irish Christians who were radiant with hope. These young people had come together to tell us Anglican bishops what our priorities should be when we meet at the Lambeth Conference in Canterbury this year. Their confidence in the future was not based on the latest news but on their refusal to succumb to the evil of violence or become the victims of fear or fatalism. The image of the young Irish Christians was so much more powerful than the images of death which their visitors had brought with them to that country. Fear gave way to a *new* and *living* hope. It had been a good place to meet.

Do not be deceived. God has assigned in Jesus Christ a good future in his world and a good destiny beyond it for those ways and works in which the Spirit of Jesus is present. And do not be deceived either that there is a very poor future in his world and no destiny at all beyond it for those ways and works which oppose the Spirit of Jesus and try to destroy it. This is the Easter hope which God had implanted in us – a hope relevant to everything, from private living to social relationships to political action. It can reshape and transform our lives if we will trust God and admit our weakness, and let his loving strength and power sustain and renew us.

I pray that each Easter morning you will rejoice and thank God we are united at the Eucharist in one unshakeable truth; that living hope which God has given us in the resurrection of Jesus Christ.

17

John Bunyan and the Christian Journey

At a tercentenary celebration of the death of John Bunyan, Robert Runcie paid tribute to the great writer who gave us, in his classic The Pilgrim's Progress, *a timeless image of the difficulties – and triumphs – of the Christian journey.*

I come here hoping that my office, as Archbishop, will sum up and focus the tribute I believe the Church of England desires to pay to John Bunyan,[1] to this great Englishman, to this outstanding literary artist, but above all to this man of God, a servant of Jesus Christ. It is indeed a tribute to the spiritual stature of the man that so many different traditions are represented at this Tercentenary celebration.

In his tract, *Christian Behaviour*,[2] Bunyan himself wrote:

> Christians are like the several flowers in a garden that bear upon each of them the dew of heaven, which being shaken with the wind, they let fall their dew at each others' roots, whereby they are nourished and become nourishers of each other.

What a fine picture that is to keep before us as we seek, under the guidance of God, to draw closer together. Indeed it is in some measure a tribute to Bunyan himself that the inter-Church process in which so many of us are currently engaged[3] should be called 'Not Strangers but Pilgrims'; for John Bunyan's greatest legacy has been to remind us that the Christian life *is* a pilgrimage. It is about movement.

1. 1628–88.
2. Published 1663.
3. To replace the British Council of Churches.

With that truth in mind, surely it is appropriate to say of John Bunyan that he was a man for whom the well-known verse from Hebrews was especially true:

> Let us lay aside every weight, and sin that clings so closely, and let us run with perseverance the race that is set before us, looking to Jesus the pioneer and perfector of our faith, who for the joy that was set before him endured the cross, despising the shame, and is seated at the right hand of the throne of God. (Heb. 12: 1–2)

It is of this calling Bunyan reminds us fundamentally. Here, as in *The Pilgrim's Progress*, is *movement*; a passing from where we are now, to where God would have us be. A pilgrimage is not a race, but look again at *The Pilgrim's Progress* and see how often Christian is depicted as *running*. There is an urgency, a single-mindedness in that image that we so need today. Let us look more closely at it.

First, *we need courage to begin the Christian journey*. You will recall how, at the very beginning of *The Pilgrim's Progress*, Christian is tempted not to embark even upon his journey by his wife, his neighbours and especially by Mr Worldly Wiseman. Is that not a temptation that we have all felt? The sheer inconvenience and unreasonableness of Christian commitment holds many back from activity. It might involve awkward explanations to family, neighbours or colleagues at work. To do it properly takes time and who has enough of that? Better to leave it until the children have grown up, or until retirement. We need courage to begin and we find that courage when we surrender our lives to God: that is the unfashionable word.

We live in a world where millions of people are seeking in so many different ways to *gain* control of their own lives. The idea of *surrendering* control is not often an attractive one. But in days when humankind has mustered so much control over outer space, there remains in the inner spaces of our lives much poverty, shallowness and confusion.

Once we surrender to God our sinful inadequacy no longer paralyses us, for God gives us a glimpse of the life of heaven.

It is the vision of the life of heaven which draws us on our journey.

Bunyan's vision of heaven was homely as well as celestial. There is some echo of Bedfordshire in the heavenly geography. In the delectable mountains he is not thinking of the archbishops or the Peak District, but the Bedfordshire hills not rising above 600 feet, yet enough to lift a man's heart. Out of the sights of home we construct our ultimate affections. And, although he gave up bell-ringing upon his conversion, it is cheering to know that his vision of heaven included the renewed ringing of bells. The celestial city would be filled with joy abounding. The courage to start this journey towards the life of heaven comes in surrender to God in the place God has given us, and among the people God has given us to love.

Secondly, *we need to know what it is to be forgiven.* Knowledge of sin as self-centredness brought Bunyan to a knowledge of the saving work of Christ. Here he was at one with John Wesley,[4] that other great spiritual visionary, whose conversion 250 years ago is being so widely celebrated this year. Wesley too, you will recall, had come to know in a new and deeper way that Christ had 'forgiven my sins, even mine'. It was that sense of God's goodness that gave Wesley, like Bunyan, a new depth in his understanding of the nature of God's love.

Bunyan describes the liberation of forgiveness in Christ movingly and eloquently:

> So I saw in my dream that just as Christian came up with the Cross, his burden loosed from off his shoulders and fell from off his back, and began to tumble, and so continued to do until it came to the mouth of the sepulchre, where it fell in, and I saw it no more.
>
> Then was Christian glad and lightsome, and said with a merry heart. 'He hath given me rest by his sorrow, and life by his death.' Then he stood awhile to look and wonder, for it was very surprising for him that the sight of the Cross should thus ease him of his burden. He looked therefore, and looked again, even till the springs that were in his head sent the waters down his cheeks.

4. 1703–91.

The experience is perhaps the most profound in human existence, but at the same time, as Christian found, surprising
in its simplicity. But we must not confuse simplicity with
shallowness. The Gospel is simple, yet it is profound. The
simplest Christians often have a greater depth of trust, charity
and faithfulness than the sophisticated. It is those qualities
in depth that the Church badly needs. Accept the fact that you
are accepted in spite of being so unacceptable; surrender
brings assurance, confidence and bread for the journey.

Then thirdly, *we must have a definite goal for our Christian journey*
– a destination nothing less than heaven itself.

Archbishop Michael Ramsey, who died recently, devoted
his life to interpreting St John's Gospel. He saw the journey
of Jesus towards the Father in adoration and into the world
in service as *one movement*; so it is for every Christian. We
move towards God in adoration and towards his world in
service.

Here too is a challenge to our living, our preaching and to
all our ministry. We live surrounded by people with no goals
in life, or mistaken goals, or positively evil goals. To them
we must speak. In *The Pilgrim's Progress* many people point
Christian onto the next stage. 'Doest thou see yonder . . . ?'
is a recurring phrase.

To guide others we must ourselves have a vision of that
goal of the Christian Life. The Orthodox Church in the Soviet
Union is very aware of heaven. Their worship is a glimpse of
glory, and that heavenly vision has done much to sustain the
Church through years of persecution. A Russian archbishop
said to me: 'I have been reading the works of one of your
theologians. He does not seem to believe in the heavenly
kingdom. How can you be a Christian and not believe in
heaven?'

The person who denies the prospect of heaven foreshortens
the perspective of life, and so acquires a false and distorted
view of it. Inevitably, he conducts his life on a short-term
policy. That is why so many political Utopias turn to persecution: all men are brothers except those who in the name
of brotherhood need to be eliminated. It is a terrible fact that
when men ignore God they cease to be fully human. It is a

terrible fact that when they deny eternity they cannot be content in time. It is a terrible fact that when they will have none of the heavenly city, they cannot build a tolerable society on earth.

Courage in surrendering to God, a sense of Christ's forgiveness of our sins, and a glimpse of the glory behind the world of time and space, these are the great truths to which Bunyan constantly recalls us in his writings. His witness is all the more remarkable, because in no sense can Bunyan be described as an escapist, one hiding from the realities of life in a religious dream. Bunyan, as we all know, was deeply involved in, and personally suffered greatly from, some of the turmoil and injustices of his day. Today we would call him an activist, a fighter for the afflicted and a prisoner of conscience. Thinking of Bunyan in Bedford jail brings to mind all who suffer unjust imprisonment.

The remarkable thing about John Bunyan is that in all his clashes with authority he never seemed a mere agitator, and he never lost sight of the call to personal holiness or the vision of the celestial city. We are too ready to see almost as alternatives involvement in issues of the day on the one hand, and high standards of personal holiness and heavenly vision, on the other. But they are *not* alternatives and we must constantly teach and show that they are not. Towards God in adoration and towards the darkness of the world in service, *the journey is one*.

John Bunyan died in London. The news reached his congregation in Bedford on 4 September 1688. They passed the day 'in prayer and humiliation for this heavy stroke upon us, the death of dear brother Bunyan.'

But for Bunyan himself the call had come, as he had described it for Mr Valiant For Truth:

Then said he, 'I am going to my Father, and though with great difficulty I am got hither yet now I do not repent me of all the trouble I have been at to arrive where I am. My sword, I give to him that shall succeed me in my pilgrimage, and my courage and skill, to him that can get it. My marks and scars I carry with me, to be a witness of me that I have fought His battles who now will be my rewarder'. When the day that he must go hence was come, many accompanied him to the riverside, into which, as he went, he said. 'Death where is thy sting?' and as he went down deeper, he said 'Grave where is thy victory?' So he passed over, and the trumpets sounded for him on the other side.

18

God's Ancient People – the Jews[1]

Suffering and forgiveness are a part of the legacy of the oppressed Jewish people – but here the Archbishop looks also at the greatness of their past, and at the healing which their hope for the future can bring.

Our memories are the touchstone of our character. The musician remembers melodies, the artist pictures, the financier figures. A place of worship, a religious building, a holy building, is always a remembering sort of place. Into a church or synagogue we bring human things – birth, marriage, death, our flickering communion with God and our fragile relationships with each other. We bring them in remembrance and, so remembering them in the light of God's laws and loving-kindness, they are deepened and shaped for the future.

We have come to this place of worship to remember those who died in two world wars, and to do so I have a text from the book of Job: 'I would seek unto God, and unto God would I commit my cause' (Job 5:8)

When our theological students first give serious attention to the Hebrew scriptures, they notice that 'Israel' is the name not only of a patriarch but also of a people. Likewise, 'Judah' is the name not only of one of that patriarch's sons but also of a kingdom. Our students realize quickly that this identification of names is no mere coincidence. The people were called Israel after the patriarch, and the kingdom Judah after one of his sons. The solidarity of the people with its past is expressed in the taking of these names.

1. Address at Remembrance Shabbat (Sabbath) at the West London Synagogue, 12 November 1988.

Our students, like most members of the Church of England, would describe themselves as English or, possibly, British. Like most Englishmen, I turn my mind at this season of remembrance to events which are within my personal memory; to colleagues who fought with me in the Second World War but who, unlike me, paid for their service to the cause with their lives or with lifelong incapacity. I remember with respect, and with a certain sadness, that they were called to pay so great a price.

Of the First World War I have no personal memory at all. And of the wars which preceded that, there are no living survivors nor even newsreels. It takes a supreme effort of will and imagination to convince myself that I have anything to do with them. Few are the Englishmen now who feel a debt of gratitude to Sir Francis Drake and his sailors or to the Dukes of Marlborough and Wellington and their soldiers. We may convince ourselves intellectually that we owe much to their costly service to this country, but we do not *feel* personally and directly in their debt.

The English simply do not have that solidarity with the past which is so characteristic of the people of Israel. Our solidarity is limited. It is largely confined to our personal remembrances. It is evident from the Scriptures that the solidarity of the ancient people of Israel with their past extended much, much further. It was felt much more intimately. The deliverance from Egypt was a present joy to generations born long afterwards. The pain of the exile was still felt centuries after the return. All the people of ancient Israel gained a share in a corporate memory which was no less poignant and emotive than each person's personal memories of joys and sorrows, triumphs and tragedies, experienced in his or her own past.

I believe this still to be true of the Jewish people today. At the forefront of your minds will be more than merely personal memories. I believe we all need to learn from this. Of course there are personal remembrances for you and for me – of friends and colleagues and members of this congregation who died in aircraft, ship and tank. Memories of parents, brothers and sisters, wives, neighbours and friends, who suffered hard-

ships, even death itself, on what was called 'the home front'.
These are the sort of memories you and I share.

We need to remember also *this country* and its national story.
Nations must have stories which tell where we have come
from, what we stand for, what we are prepared to die for and
where we are going. War is a fertile breeding ground for
stories like this. They help to describe and determine the
dedication and pride every country needs. Countries, like
individuals, only prosper if they are loved. We need to remember how much we owe to other people who gave their lives
or their health or their future in war. Nowadays we are
inclined to be cynical or embarrassed about heroism. But a
person who has convinced himself that everyone is second-
rate is usually content to be second-rate himself. So we give
thanks for our nation and we give thanks for its good
examples.

Of course at the centre of the corporate Jewish memory in
this generation stands the appalling horror of the holocaust.
I comprehend the magnitude of that horror. You *feel* it. You
experience it today almost as if you had been present whilst
those dreadful things were done. For many it is the evil in
the world which prevents them believing in God. I cannot
avoid addressing that question at remembrance-tide. Then
too there is a second question. What can a Christian archbishop say to a congregation of Jewish people who live with
the memory of the war and of the holocaust?

First, the problem of evil. How could God tolerate the
Sommes, the Paschendaels, the Stalingrads, Belsen, Auschwitz, Hiroshima? We can only say that the question is as old
as mankind, and so is the answer. In the words of Isaiah,
'Shall the clay say unto him that fashioned it, What makest
thou? Or thy work, Thou has no hands?' (Isa. 45:9). Both
question and answer thunder through the dialogue in the
Book of Job, where God turns the question back on the
questioner in that tremendous interrogation. He describes the
full majesty and wonder of his creation to the wretched human
being who had been complaining of his private misery and
asked him what *he* knew about it. 'Where wast thou when I
laid the foundations of the earth . . . when the morning stars

together sang and all the sons of God shouted for joy?' (Job 38:4,7).

Who are we to seek to know the ultimate purposes of God? To ask why he allows wars to happen is like asking why he allows crime or tyranny or disease or famine? Indeed why does he allow history to happen at all? Why does he allow love to happen, or joy, or loyalty, or integrity? Fundamentally, it is the same question. The world is not made neutral nor neutered.

We believe, both as Jews and Christians, that God works *within* the human predicament, and uses it for his own purposes. He even uses suffering, perhaps indeed particularly suffering. Perhaps one of Job's comforters had it right when he said, 'Those who suffer he rescues through suffering' (Job 36:15). Without suffering there is no redemption, no salvation, perhaps indeed no peace. The suffering people of Israel long knew this. The Jewish people during this century have known it too. And Christians, for their part, have long gazed at the cross as the place of redemptive suffering.

Christians look to the cross as a place to seek forgiveness. Which brings me to the second question I believe a Christian archbishop must answer on remembrance shabbat. Can I say *anything* to your corporate memory – a memory which includes not only the holocaust but a multitude of other wrongs which Jews have suffered at the hands of Christians? To ask for your forgiveness might be proper, but too easy a gesture. The wrongs done are too great and too many for such simple and facile atonement. So I offer you what is more than a gesture. I offer you a hope and a prayer – a prayer that by the mercy of God the corporate memory of Israel may be *healed*.

We know that personal memories can be healed. I can recall things in my past which once filled me with rage or guilt. Now some, when I remember them, no longer do so. This is not because someone who wronged me has apologized nor because I have said sorry to someone I have treated badly. The healing has to come about, inexplicably, because I see certain things in a different perspective. Why should it be? How could it be? Rather, working through time, I sense an unfolding, gentle, healing graciousness. It is the same divine graciousness which heals, slowly and imperceptibly, the scars we inflict on the world of nature. It is the divine graciousness which heals scarred memories of past events. It does not extinguish our personal memories. We should *never* forget, but God desires us to live without the constant, searing pain which is a denial of his creative goodness. God, in his mercy, spares us from living forever with the worst things which we have suffered or done.

At the outbreak of the last war a man called Leonard Wilson[2] was our bishop in Singapore. He became a prisoner in the infamous Changi jail. There he suffered, with thousands of others, brutal and relentless torture. But he never lost hope or faith. He tried to follow the example of Jesus of Nazareth and prayed for God's forgiveness for his torturers. After the war he came back to this country to be a much loved Bishop of Birmingham. But in 1948 he was allowed to return to Singapore. There he held a confirmation service in his old cathedral. At confirmation, the bishop lays his hands on the head of each candidate and prays that God's Holy Spirit will be poured upon them. Suddenly amongst the candidates he saw one of the most sadistic of his torturers. A wave of fear swept over him as their eyes met. But Leonard Wilson laid hands on his former jailer and afterwards they talked and embraced. The man told him how hard he found it to live with his memories of giving those beatings. The bishop told the man how hard he had found it to live with the memories of being beaten. Yet in and through God's graciousness something even greater than forgiveness was at work – the healing of memories and the gift of new life and hope.

Personal memories can be, and are, healed. The healing of corporate memories must be more protracted. Yet it cannot be beyond the bounds of possibility that the same graciousness which heals our personal memories may heal the memories of a people also. And for that I pray on this day of remembrance: that, by the mercy of God, the Jewish people may be enabled to live without pain with *all* their past.

Healing is the reawakening of hope. The Jewish people have been tragically and fearfully wounded in this and earlier

2. John Leonard Wilson 1887–1970; appointed Bishop of Singapore 1941, of Birmingham 1953.

centuries. As a people, you bear those wounds. But open wounds which are scratched sap the body's energy and life. I pray that the wounds of your past may, by God's gracious act, be healed. They will not disappear. The scars of your suffering will remain. But I pray that they will not diminish your life now but that, *despite all*, you will know the hope and joy in God which comes through his healing.

Remembrance is solemn. We, as a nation, recognize the scars of war inflicted on so many of our families. But in remembering, we help to heal by rekindling hope, a hope the more impressive for its lack of show.

I am glad that our remembrance ceremonies have never been the occasion of triumphant parades or great patriotic demonstrations. We built no Arc de Triomphe or Victory Pillar to commemorate the fact we won the Great War; only a Cenotaph, an empty tomb to remind us of the price of victory. The military leaders received their usual rewards but the place of highest honour was reserved for an unknown soldier to represent so many millions who suffered and died. We sing no rousing battle songs. Instead whether at Cenotaph or Synagogue we renew our faith in a God whose purposes are unfathomable, whose power is infinite, but in whose grace and healing love we place our abiding trust. That is a way of remembering which the ancient people of Israel would have recognized. It is faithful to the message of the Hebrew scriptures. It is a reflection of an unswerving trust in God and his promises, *whatever happens*, which finds its origins in the faith of God's ancient people, the Jews.

19

Kristallnacht[1]

The Archbishop shares with the Jewish community the remembrance of Kristallnacht – the infamous night of 9th November 1938, when Jewish shops, offices, homes and synagogues were destroyed by Nazi sympathizers.

The remembrance of Kristallnacht is primarily a Jewish event. That is why I am so deeply moved by the invitation to share with you the memory of Jewish suffering. In the final days of the last war, I was a soldier and was among the first troops to enter the Belsen concentration camp. When people asked me whether I regret my part in fighting, I have often replied, 'The war closed down Belsen and Auschwitz.'

But I recognize that we did *not* go to war to close down the concentration camps. Indeed we, and most other nations, had closed our frontiers to all but a small number of those seeking asylum. The desperate search of many for visas led, literally, to a dead end. We went to war to prevent Germany dominating the whole of Europe. In 1938 Adolf Hitler was already the absolute ruler of the German nation, Austria included. He made it clear that he wanted to erase from Germany all that, in his madness, he chose to describe as 'alien blood'. That much was known. The Munich agreement was but one sign of a great conspiracy of silence and complicity which leaves its legacy of shame.

Kristallnacht has its origins deep in the history of Christian Europe. Without centuries of Christian anti-semitism, Hitler's

1. Address at the Kristallnacht Memorial Meeting held on 9 November 1988 at Friends House, Euston Road, London.

passionate hatred would never have been so fervently echoed. In his home town of Linz there had been very few Jews, but living in Vienna he developed this phobia. In *Mein Kampf*[2] his twisted hatred was expressed in the language of an established and perverse tradition:

> Was there any shady undertaking, any form of foulness, especially in cultural life, in which at least one Jew did not participate?

This horrid perception of the Jew festered in Hitler's mind. Once the Nazis gained control of German government in 1933, Jews were eliminated from the civil service, the legal and medical professions, and cultural and educational institutions. And then, on November 9th, 1938, came Kristallnacht. The news was not kept secret from the outside world. Two days later *The New York Times* reported:

> A wave of destruction and looting swept over Germany as National Socialist cohorts took vengeance on Jewish shops, offices and synagogues. Huge, but mostly silent, crowds looked on, and the police confined themselves to regulating traffic and making wholesale arrests of Jews. In some communities every male Jew was sent to a concentration camp.

Earlier this year I paid a visit to Berlin. There I saw the site of the synagogue in Fasenenstrasse, one of the first to be smashed to pieces. We cannot say, 'we did not know'. We did know, and we stood aside. There are painful reminders of our negligence all over Germany. Cain's eternal question rings out: 'Am I my brother's keeper?'

Nazi barbarism resulted in the construction of the death camps in which six million Jews perished. Tonight, as we remember Kristallnacht, the beginning of the acceleration of the process by which Germany determined on genocide, I want to speak about three things. The first is to acknowledge the guilty silence of the churches then, both within and without Germany. The second is to ask how we can honour God and trust Him after the holocaust. And thirdly, I want to say

2. Literally 'My Struggle'; first published 1923.

how I believe the tragic events of the holocaust have altered the relationship of Christians to Jews.

First, the silence of the churches. Although individual pastors expressed their disapproval of the excesses of Kristallnacht, church leaders said little. A good many expressed the view that whilst the violence was extreme, it was understandable because of the harm the Jews were doing and had long done to the German economy and way of life. The Confessing Church, the only continuing opposition to Hitler's German Christians, was beginning to lose its way. Karl Barth was right when he said in retrospect:

> Bonhoeffer[3] was the first, indeed almost the only theologian, who in the years after 1933 concentrated energetically on the question of the Jews and dealt with it equally energetically. For a long time now I have considered myself guilty of not having raised it with equal emphasis during the Church struggle.

Dietrich Bonhoeffer was attending a retreat at the time of the Kristallnacht. But as soon as he heard the news of what had happened, he wrote to his students and urged them to read Psalm 74. In his own Bible that Psalm is marked and underlined. Every time I read that Psalm in our own Prayer Book it reminds me of the events of Kristallnacht, so accurately does it seem to be prefigured there.

> Thine adversaries roar in the midst of they congregations: and set up their banners for tokens.
> . . . now they break down all the carved work thereof: with axes and hammers.
> They have set fire upon thy holy places: and have defiled the dwelling place of thy name, even unto the ground.

The travesty of Kristallnacht and all that followed is that so much was perpetrated in Christ's name. To glorify the Third Reich, the Christian faith was betrayed. The slaughter of the Jews was a desecration of the ministry of Jesus, himself a Jew.

Neither inside nor outside Germany did the Churches

---

3. 1906–45; German Protestant theologian and pastor, executed 1945.

recognize this. And even today there are many Christians who fail to see it as self-evident. And why this blindness? Because for centuries Christians have held Jews collectively responsible for the death of Jesus. On Good Friday Jews have, in times past, cowered behind locked doors for fear of a Christian mob seeking 'revenge' for deicide. Without the poisoning of Christian minds through the centuries, the holocaust is unthinkable.

In his teaching, Jesus continually stressed that those who loved God were to do good to all without distinction; they were to forgive all, just as they had been forgiven; they were to respond to the call of need, whatever its origins. And that ethic of love was to extend even to one's enemies. This was to be the sign of the unfolding of God's kingdom on earth. When we recall the gas chambers and the mass graves of the holocaust we see the extent to which that vision of universal love was betrayed. We see why Christians can only meditate on the nightmare of Kristallnacht and the Nazi era with a profound sense of grief.

Which brings me to the question – how can we honour God and trust him after the holocaust?

God *is* dishonoured but he is *not* dethroned. The distinguished Jewish theologian, Emil Fackenheim,[4] has eloquently and urgently expressed this conviction. Through the holocaust, he believes, God issued the 614th commandment: Jews are forbidden to grant posthumous victories to Hitler. They are forbidden to despair of God or of the world as the place of his just and gentle rule. For Fackenheim it is a betrayal of the Jewish heritage to question whether the traditional Jewish belief in God can be sustained after the holocaust. Fackenheim believes it important to recognize the *religious* significance of the Jewish refusal to give up hope. Pregnant mothers refused to abort their pregnancies, hoping their offspring would survive and frustrate Nazi plans to eliminate every Jew. Hassidic Jews prayed though they were forbidden to do so. Only by affirming life and maintaining dignity could the desire for destruction be defeated.

4. Emil Ludwig Fackenheim, born Germany 1916; became Canadian. Professor, Department of Philosophy, University of Toronto.

Fackenheim's message is of course directed primarily to the Jewish community. The 614th commandment is added to the 613 other commandments in the Torah. But it is a message for the Christian community too. We also must not allow Hitler – or that-of-Hitler in each of us – to have any posthumous victories. The Jewish people form part of God's plan for his world, and it is our responsibility not merely to ensure their survival – God has done that – but that they are honoured and respected and loved.

Which brings me to my third point. A new understanding of Christian-Jewish relationships emerges from all this. The Jewish people are the people of God, those who bestowed to us the Hebrew scriptures, who gave the Christian world so much of its heritage of faith. Jewish wisdom and Jewish prophecy have been a light to us and will continue to be a light to the nations, even when Jews fall short, as we all do, of their highest ideals.

God's voice also calls us today as Christians to remember and honour the martyrs of the holocaust. So many Jews met persecution, suffering and death in a truly religious spirit. We have our own martyrs – Christians who perished in their solidarity with the Jewish people. Let Maximilian Kolbe and Maria Skobotsova stand for them all alongside Dietrich Bonhoeffer – Catholic friar, Orthodox nun, and Lutheran pastor. They must not be forgotten. But neither must we forget that even though there were a few great churchmen, like Heinrich Gruber who set up rescue organizations and survived to become Provost of Berlin, many Jews knew that it was Christians who pushed them into the gas chambers. It is no good saying they were not *real* Christians any more than we should say those who did not go regularly to synagogue were not *real* Jews. In the light of all that, how can we in our generation go to the Jewish people and say, without shame, 'You have rejected your Messiah,' or, 'We have the truth, listen to us'. We cannot pretend that recent history has not happened.

Christians have much to learn from the ancient people of God in interpreting their own gospel. Our Christian faith is not shaken by discovering how much Jews have to give us in extending our understanding of God. In particular, many Christian ministers who have had the privilege of discussing

the Bible with Jewish scholars will testify how much they
have gained from it.

Our task as Christians is to hold sincerely to our faith in
Christ and to speak of our desire to be conformed to his life,
death and resurrection. This discipleship of Jesus of Nazareth,
Jews can understand and respect. Hectoring from a position
of spiritual superiority they cannot. Nor should they. With St
Paul we must recognize that it is God alone who can bring
us all into one fold.

As we remember the streets of Germany, littered with
broken glass, we must not simply despair of the past. Neither
is it enough either merely to *understand* the events leading to
the gas chambers. What lies before us is the task of creating
a world in which such tragedies do not take place again. The
planned destruction of the Jewish people did not succeed.
Out of suffering God brought a new-found liberty. As we
Christians would say, out of death he brought resurrection.
Out of the pogroms of Russia, God brought new-found liberty
for Jews in the United States. He also brought new-found
liberty for Jews in Israel.

The sacrificial victims of the death camps must live in our
memories. These memories commit us to all in our world who
are outcast, homeless, hungry and oppressed. We honour the
victims of yesterday by standing alongside the victims of
today. Our love goes out to the ancient and young nation of
Israel, to the people of the Holy Land, Jews, Muslims and
Christians alike, who are *all* God's children and neighbours
to be loved. We must hearken to the divine command which
rings out from the ghettoes and the concentration camps.
With one voice we must insist: *Never again!* The Lord our God
is one, to be loved with all our mind and heart and soul, and
our neighbour as ourself.

20

The Chapel, Lambeth Palace[1]

The Chapel is one of the great glories of Lambeth Palace. Here the Archbishop delights in its restoration, but also shows how much more this is than just a beautiful building.

Woven silently into the new altar cloth of the renovated chapel are the words of T. S. Eliot,

> Light
> The visible reminder of Invisible Light.[2]

It is always a delicate thing, this matter of the invisible made visible. Most often the deepest truth has been there quietly all the time waiting for something to open human eyes to it. We see it – and, in the words of the same poet, 'Know the place for the first time.'[3]

Our charge in this restoration of Lambeth Palace Chapel has been to recover its mystery and its memory. The chapel's destruction by incendiary bombs in the Second World War damaged both. The roof was destroyed; so was the glass; much of the timber was reduced to ash. After the war a courageous restoration was completed in 1955. But there were limits to what could be achieved then.

Now we have done three things. First, we have reintroduced Archbishop Laud's screen, much of which miraculously survived the bombing. It now stands again where it did when

1. Address at a service of thanksgiving for the restoration of Lambeth Palace chapel, 2 November 1988.
2. T. S. Eliot, *Collected Poems 1909–1962* (Faber and Faber 1963), Choruses from 'The Rock', ix, p. 182.
3. Ibid., 'Four Quartets', Little Gidding, v, p. 222.

he said his prayers here before being taken down the river to the Tower of London, to imprisonment and execution, just before the English Civil War. Secondly, the ceiling which in the past had been a colourful feature of this chapel, has been painted by a contemporary artist, not in slavish imitation of previous decoration, but as a means to recall the chapel's history. And in the painting that history is directed towards Christ, the Church's living head. Thirdly, we have made this chapel more evidently a focus for the Anglican Communion, by re-ordering the stalls so that the Primate of each Province may have a place here. The first service upon this chapel's reopening happened the day before the Lambeth Conference began, when all the Primates of the Anglican Communion came to occupy their stalls. Here they gathered where so many of their predecessors had been consecrated for their mission. Here Asian, African, American and European bishops joined to express their unity in Christ and in the Anglican tradition.

So here we have taken what is old and venerable, like the screen of William Laud, and *re*-made it. And yet, each new age does not merely remake history, but creates it. So there is creativity in this restoration – a looking outwards to the world beyond these borders, where most Anglicans now live. Our appreciation of the past moves us to mission in the future.

But above all, this chapel is a place of devotion. In a holy place the power of sacred association penetrates deeply into human hearts. Coming into this place you do not enter into silence simply, for silence can be dead. You move rather into stillness – coming through the screen you must let the mystery of stillness disclose itself. Movement, life, can be gathered into stillness; that is the difference between silence and the poet's stillness.

There is a design here to convey to others, even to the casual visitor, the meaning of a place where that most hidden movement of all movements, the movement of the human heart towards God, has been made day in and day out, year in and year out; where the Eucharist has been celebrated and the Offices said. The decoration of the ceiling is not primarily to be studied as a series of pictures. It is part of the creation of an atmosphere; but it does disclose an inner mystery. The painter has hinted at the movement of which I have spoken – hinted, no more – in the movement of human hands.

Becket stands, hands tensed, before the blow that will kill him. His blood, like that of the martyrs before him, will prove to be the seed of the Church. Our Anglican Communion has again and again been reminded of this truth by the martyrs of Uganda, Kenya, Burma, South Africa, Papua New Guinea. Here in this chapel, *their* chapel, is a present mystery.

And then Matthew Parker. We see him clad red-robed; not for martyrdom, but for faithfulness. We see him pensive before the moment of his consecration as a bishop, hand lifted, somehow between a blessing, and a hand laid upon the mouth before speaking a mystery. Here are the same hands then clasped in submission, as other hands lay on him the burden of the office of a bishop. And then these same hands of his become strong and confident as he dispenses the rods of administration to those on whom he will rely. Day by day our brothers over the world accept again, know again, share again, that same burden.

Their Primates came to Lambeth in 1988, and their symbols now wait in their stalls for each succeeding visit. But, more than that, their symbols gather them quietly, at every moment, into the remembrance of this place. They remind those of us who worship here of their people, of all that they suffer and all that they have to do. And our own hands of prayer reaching out to them gather us all together to that fine point of the stillness of this place where humanity is held and remade, in the crucified and risen Lord of glory, the Head of his Church, Christ the King. He is the visible reminder of Invisible Light; the Lord of all Creation.

We give thanks for the hands that have made and remade this Chapel. On the west wall the hand of Gregory points Augustine to this our beloved land where the mystery of Invisible Light is still at work and in our world; the mystery of Christ's renewing love, ever waiting for eyes and hearts to be opened to receive it.

21

Christmas

A Christmas message[1] which celebrates not only the joys of the season, but which looks more deeply at the meaning which the birth of Christ has for all humanity.

In these last days God has spoken to us by His Son. (Heb. 1:2)

Down the centuries men and women have heard the Christmas message come to them in these words. It comes to us at the darkest time of the year, when the countryside seems bleak and bare. It comes to us when, in the closing weeks of 1988, one human disaster has followed another: famine in the Sudan, flood in Bangladesh, earthquake in Armenia,[2] and then at home the Clapham rail crash[3] and the Lockerbie air tragedy.[4] We have been stunned by these reminders of the fragility of the world and our uncertain hold on life within it.

The message of Christmas is that God enters into our fragility. He comes with mercy and pity as a little child. It is a message of hope for our so serious a world.

Jesus called on us to read the signs of our time, to detect the traces of his coming Kingdom in the world about us. Surely one such sign for us is the amazing outpouring of compassion and giving drawn from us by the sufferings of others. Just when it seems that we are becoming complacent in our comfort, terrible tragedies disturb our selfishness and

1. Address in Canterbury Cathedral on Christmas Day 1988.
2. 7 December 1988.
3. 12 December 1988.
4. 20 December 1988.

create a response which is instant, generous and imaginative. Out of the darkness of suffering comes the light of a remarkable affirmation of our common humanity.

Thinking of recent weeks, at one moment President Gorbachev was making his significant speech to the United Nations, and the next came the news of the Armenian earthquake with its clear call to Western hearts and consciences. Suddenly hostility and suspicion were laid aside and we concentrated on treating one another as human beings. In the response, to both that speech and that disaster, were to be seen not just unilateral giving, but a mutual giving and receiving.

I recall a haunting film of a Midnight Mass being celebrated in Nagasaki at the Christmas following the dropping of the atom bomb. The bewilderment on the faces of the worshippers was unmistakeable. So too was the inspiration of their faith triumphing over circumstance. I was reminded of that on a lovely summer evening this year in Canterbury when bishops from Japan, Burma and China, old enemies, gave and planted on our university campus a Tree of Peace to commemorate the day the bomb dropped.

It is giving which helps the human spirit triumph over circumstance. But giving by itself is not enough. With it must go a willingness to receive and to give back in return. One-way giving can be destructive. The instant provision of necessary food to a disaster area is good but, if it continues indefinitely, the recipients begin to suffer debilitating dependency. None of us wants to be forever living on the hand-outs of others. So creative giving to the homeless or the handicapped has always to be directed towards the goal of allowing recipients to regain dignity and independence. We rightly celebrate generous giving in our world as a sign of grace. But we must know too how to receive as well as how to give.

That lesson is learned every Christmas in our simple, even comic, giving and receiving of presents. The Christmas cynics say we would save our time and energy by calling a truce and declining to hand over these odd items of dubious value, what John Betjeman called, 'The sweet and silly Christmas things, bath salts and inexpensive scent and hideous tie so kindly meant.'[5]

Perhaps these little extravagances do seem trivial and self-indulgent in so serious a world, but in these Christmas rituals I believe we provide a focus for the daily giving and receiving of ordinary life. Here we may learn not only to live by delighting to give, but also to live by being able graciously to receive. On Christmas Day we can become as little children, forgetting our pride and learning to tear open our parcels with eagerness.

In doing so we are to remember God's greatest gift to his world: the gift of his presence. See with what gentleness that gift is made. See in what form and circumstance he gives his presence to the world. The form is a new-born child: the circumstance a cold and lowly stable. What gift could be less hurtful to the world's pride than this? What gift could be more gladly and easily received? For here there is a perfect balance between giving and receiving, between generosity and need. The child is given for the world's need: but like any tiny baby he immediately cries out. He has needs which must be met. The child appeals to our parental instinct to give protection, care and love. The child is a gift whom parents are glad to receive and to whom they are glad to give.

In the fragile child of Bethlehem, God gives to the world the sublime gift of his presence. In the babe in the manger, 'God has spoken to us by his Son'. He has *disclosed* himself in the child's weakness. His fragility draws the strength of our love. For God has the need to receive from those who receive him. God so loves the world that he has need of its answering love: God so expends himself for the world that he has a need of its responsive service. In God there is the possibility of receiving as well as giving: in his beloved world there is the possibility of giving to him as well as receiving from him.

Mary gives to God the sheer hard work of motherhood. Tradition has it that the shepherds came, like the wise men, with gifts for the Christ Child. The God who gives us no less than himself becomes the recipient of all we have to give.

5. 'Christmas' in John Betjeman, *Collected Poems* (John Murray 1970), p. 188–9.

Here is the heart of the gladness of Christmas. This, our faith insists, is what God is always like.

On a hillside overlooking Nazareth today, outside a convent chapel, there is a terra-cotta statue of the Virgin and child: Mary is shown, not hugging the baby to herself (as instinct would have it) but gently and humbly presenting him to us. And he has his small hands extended eagerly towards the world. The vision of that sculptor is a true one. It is a perfect expression of God's generosity. We who are given his Son are drawn to give ourselves to him in return.

Christmas is about giving. Wise parents with tiny children begin to prepare them for Christmas by telling them of the lovely things they will receive. But then, within a year or two, they are helping them find ways in which they can also give. So, early on Christmas morning in countless houses, an eager, shining face and an incomprehensible picture inscribed illegibly 'to Mum and Dad', 'to my big brother', or even 'to the cat', will be presented. And Mum and Dad do not just pretend to be grateful – they *are* grateful. From the child whom they love they *need* this first fumbling expression of his or her love for them. To have no need of that love, or not be able to receive it, leaves the action of love incomplete. Just as there is nothing incomplete or possessive in our love for each other, so there is nothing incomplete or possessive about God's love for us.

Why, in so serious a world, do I find my heart strangely lifted? Why do I find in myself a new hopefulness and confidence for a message that can transform the world. The confidence in men and women receiving it gladly?

It is because I have seen so many signs of a new surge of generosity, new signs of a readiness to give and receive; a new touching of the hearts of men and women towards those whose world they share.

I have seen it in the swift and generous response to the disasters in Armenia, Clapham and Lockerbie. I have been moved too by the imaginative response to our appeals to reverse the decline and despair of urban black spots. I think also of an evening when across all the frontiers of faith we gathered to remember the sufferings that began for Jews in

Europe fifty years ago.[6] Or again, I think of the worldwide warmth of remembrance for hostages in the Lebanon and the opening up of fresh determination to deal with the injustices of that region.

I think too of the unease of thoughtful people when they ponder the fragility of the created order in which the Scriptures so firmly put the birth of Christ. As we listen to those who speak the new language of the 'greenhouse effect' or the 'ozone layer' it is as if the world he so wonderfully made is saying, 'Gently, friend; gently, please.' Here too the giving and receiving of Christmas has its message.

For a world in danger in so many ways we need more than the removal of obstacles or the search for culprits. We need the proper sharing of gifts. In thankfulness to God for Christmas, may we so learn to give that others may receive, and so learn to receive that others may give. Then we shall know that 'in these last days God has spoken to us in his Son' (Heb. 1:2).

6. See chapter 19.

22

Christians in Russia

In his annual Christmas address[1] to the people of Russia via the BBC's Russian service, the Archbishop rejoices in the new freedom of Russian Christians.

The thoughts and prayers of many Western Christians were with the Russian Orthodox Church during 1988. It was a time of new hope and commitment. A time of profound thanksgiving for the thousand years of Christianity in Russian lands. And a time when the Church could once again begin to look forward to mission and service in a rapidly changing Soviet society at the beginning of a new millennium of Christianity.

Although new opportunities to be the Church of Jesus Christ come sometimes as a surprise – and even from surprising places and people – this should not really surprise us. For our God is a God of surprises. The message of the Angel Gabriel came as a surprise to Mary the Mother of the Lord. But she was obedient. The message of the heavenly host was a surprise to the simple shepherds. But they did as they were commanded. The message of the star came as a surprise to the Magi, yet they followed it.

When I visited 'holy' Russia for the Millennium Celebrations, I was surprised and delighted how much things had changed since my previous visit a number of years ago. And they will continue to change in both wider Soviet society as *perestroika*[2] is actually put into practice and also within the

1. December 1988.
2. Restructuring.

Christian community as the Church grasps and develops the opportunities now beginning to open up for believers. Like Mary, the shepherds, and the wise men, the Church is both surprised and obedient to God's new initiatives.

During my visit to Russia in 1988 I naturally went to Kiev, the place of the baptism of St Vladimir.[3] And I visited the Lavra of the Caves – that most holy place for all Russian Christians. I was present when the ancient monastery was handed back to the Church, and I rejoiced with the Church. I was also delighted and surprised that there was already a strong community of monks ready and waiting to return to the Lavra of the Caves. The Church was prepared to grasp immediately the opportunity set before it.

As the years of the second millennium of Christianity in Russian lands begins there will be other ways in which the Church will be called to witness to the light of Christ within Soviet society. Old churches are now being reopened; new churches are being built. Of course, some difficulties remain but from what I saw I do not think there can be an easy reversal of the new directions.

Alongside the opening of new churches there may well be fresh opportunities for a wider pastoral ministry of service in the community. The Russian Orthodox Church has long been used to complementing the Soviet Union's search for peace through international Christian conferences. Now is the time for the Church to seek to complement the building up of a peace and harmony at a more local level, for no government in any country can now do without the ministry of the Church to those on the margins of society. I see this in my own country and in yours.

Another surprise is the deep hunger of so many young people for the spiritual teachings of the Church. This presents a fresh challenge: to explain the meaning of Christian faith to those who have until now been outside the Church. When I was in Russia I heard of many places where there are many adult inquirers for baptism. Here is God's surprise for the future.

The thoughts and prayers of the world are at the present

3. 956–1015; Apostle of the Russians.

time with people in the Soviet Union. Not only because of their Millennium of Christianity, and not only because of the new hopes for peace and reconciliation between East and West associated with the initiatives of Mikhail Gorbachev. The terrible tragedy of the Armenian earthquake[4] also focuses the view of the world upon you. It is one of the paradoxes of the human condition that it takes a disaster of such magnitude to bring the peoples of the world together in profound human sympathy.

The feast of Christ's birth reminds us that God, the Eternal Word, has also come in sympathy – 'to suffer with us' is the original meaning of that word. We rejoice, in spite of the sufferings of the world, that God has come among us and suffers with us. For that is the surprise of all God's surprises – the Word-made-flesh.

4. 7 December 1988.

23

The New Year[1]

A midnight broadcast which reaches out from Canterbury Cathedral to embrace the whole country, and speaks to churchgoers and non-church-goers alike. As he welcomes the New Year, the Archbishop leads us back to the centrality and the stability of God's love for the whole world.

From my home at Canterbury, I am very close to the soaring towers and arches of the great cathedral; beautiful always, but hauntingly beautiful when, as now, they are floodlit under the night sky.

I am often away from home. My journeys bring me the good fortune to meet an enormous variety of people and to experience the kindness of their hospitality. But I should not enjoy my travels if I had no home to which to return. The homeless are always travelling, but it brings them no joy to have no place to call their own. We all need a fixed point where faces are well known and things familiar, places where we belong, where we know our bearings. Without such a point of stillness, a life of constant movement would be a nightmare.

It is the thought of that sort of nightmare in a world of increasing movement which makes me grateful for people who stay put. Perhaps you are one of those who stays put by choice. Or maybe you stay put because your work or infirmity or lack of money limits your freedom of movement. If so, you may feel hemmed in by home. But there is another way of looking at this.

1. Message broadcast on BBC 1 at midnight as the New Year 1989 began.

The stay-at-homes can be found when they are wanted or needed. They become points of contact between others who are moving about in all directions. They become repositories of news. They give character to a village or district and make it a community rather than a transit camp. The world of the stay-at-homes is smaller than that of the traveller, but perhaps they see more deeply into it and gain a wisdom as valuable as the broadening of the mind, which is said to be the result of travel.

I once knew a woman who was housebound and lived several storeys up in a block of flats. There was such brightness and joy about her that all who visited her, whether to deliver the paper or the milk, to show the new baby or collect her pools coupon, grew to appreciate and love her. In her flat these people would meet one another. They took messages from her to neighbours. Friendship and mutual caring grew around her. It was even noted that there was little vandalism and higher morale in that block. Though stuck at home that lady helped to create a community. Her home was not just for herself, but for others.

Canterbury Cathedral is the home of English Christianity. It does not exist for itself, but for others. Here millions of tourists and pilgrims come; during 1988 bishops from all over the world gathered here. Here within the Cathedral we set in the floor a compass rose. Its points radiate from the spiritual home of Anglicans to the parts of our world where we are dispersed. Some of our bishops returned to homely, secure situations. Others went back to the Sudan, Northern Ireland, South Africa, Bangladesh, the Middle East, Burma – to face uncertainty and unrest, famine and flood. Yet for each of them this cathedral was and is a fixed point, a holy place reminding them that amidst restless uncertainty there is security in God. He holds all things together.

Each of us, whether a traveller or a stay-at-home, needs a still centre where we sense the things that hold life together. The world needs its innovators and pioneers, relishing new challenges and opportunities, even stimulated by uncertainty. But it needs also its stabilizers, the people who keep us rooted, the home-makers and home-builders.

God is leading us always into new ways, but he is also

the stabilizer, holding us secure in his love. To that God Canterbury Cathedral bears witness. That is why it can lift human hearts and hopes. It has stood over the centuries for what a poet[2] calls 'Light/The visible reminder of Invisible Light'. That is what we need when so much of the news is dark. At the New Year I leave you with some words written seven centuries ago.

> There is no stopping place in this life. No, nor was there ever one for anyone, no matter how far along the way they've come. This, then, above all things: Be ready for the gifts of God, and always for new ones.[3]

2. T. S. Eliot, in Choruses from 'The Rock', *Collected Poems 1909–1962*, Faber and Faber, 1963.
3. Meister Eckhart (*c.* 1260–1327).